Alexander Tzonis

LE CORBUSIER
THE POETICS OF MACHINE AND METAPHOR

Thames & Hudson

In memoriam
Shadrach Woods and Edith Aujame, who worked with Le
Corbusier; Gavin Borden, President of Garland Publishing,
who published the Archive; and Alexandros Tzonis, Architect

First published in the United Kingdom in 2001 by
Thames & Hudson Ltd, 181A High Holborn, London WC1V 7QX

British Library Cataloguing-in-Publication Data
A catalogue record for this book is available from the British Library

ISBN 0-500-283-192

Printed and bound in Bath, England by Bath Press
.

Design: Joseph Cho and Stefanie Lew, Binocular, New York
Universe Editor: Terence Maikels
Copy Editor: Laura Magzis

Frontispiece: Villa Savoye, Poissy, France,
photograph by Michael Levin

CONTENTS

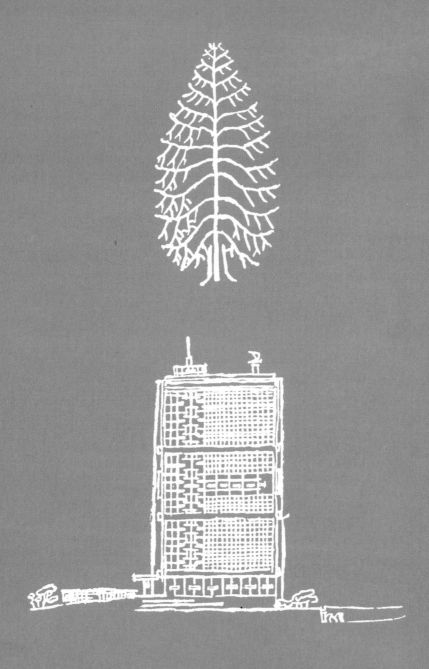

"Everything Is Architecture"

Rather than accepting received categories of buildings and design conventions, Le Corbusier redesigned architectural beliefs and desires of his time by declaring that *"everything is architecture."* By that he meant that one could recruit knowledge to create new artefacts from every existing object and that one has the possibilities and the responsibilities to make architecture in every product rather than a select shortlist. The present monograph discusses Le Corbusier's œuvre in a concise global manner in relation to the revolutionary technological, cultural, socio-economic, and political movements of his time. It explores how within this context the particular cognitive capacities, the unique spatial intelligence, and the collective memory with which Le Corbusier was endowed enabled him to develop a unique poetics of *machine* and *metaphor*, radically changing the way people see, use, and make their architecture. However, the same conditions, historical, contextual, and cognitive, that nurtured the invention of new spaces blocked also the new; bred illusions and biases; and caused unanticipated, unintended, and unwanted failures. Thus, Le Corbusier as the *architect* of *modern life* tells us much about the power and constraints of creativity as well as the fiascos and achievements of the twentieth century.

Books and articles on Le Corbusier are a real industry. Given the quantity and unequal quality of this huge production, becoming acquainted with his work becomes increasingly difficult. However, I would like to draw the attention of the reader to the writings of Jean Petit, Paul Turner, Allen Brooks, Eduard and Patricia Sekler, William Curtis, W. Treib, Michael Danièle Pauly, Jean-Louis Cohen, Brian Taylor, Gilles Ragot, and Mathilde Dion. The titles of their books are in the bibliography at the end of this book. Certainly, as is every researcher or amateur of Le Corbusier's work, I am grateful to Le Corbusier himself as "editor-author" of the *Œuvre Complète*. Last but not least I would like to mention here *The Le Corbusier Archive*, edited by Allen Brooks, of the Garland Architectural Archive series that I directed as General Editor.

The beginnings of this book go back to the years immediately after World War II, when Volume One of Le Corbusier's *Œuvre* was given to my grandfather. I discussed with him for the first time architecture. A pragmatic Thessalonikian architect who had just retired, he did not have many good things to say about the realized or the visionary projects in the book. For me, however, I was just ten years old then, the book made my "eyes see." I never met Le Corbusier, however, throughout the years I had the very good luck to be in constant contact with people who were very close to him as collaborators and friends. This book indeed would have been impossible without the intellectual support and friendship of, in particular, Lucien Hervé and Shadrach Woods, who shared many of their ideas about Le Corbusier with me. I am also grateful to Judith Hervé, Jerzy Soltan, Jean-Louis Veret, Edith and Roger Aujame, and W. Boesinger, who devoted a whole day, just before his death, discussing the genesis and development of the *Œuvre* series.

Grille CIAM d'Urbanisme, book cover

Part of this book was presented during the series of lessons I offered in May 2001 at the College de France. I express my gratitude to Professor Jacques Glowinski for this unique opportunity. Although in its final phase, the book profited from the companionship I found there, I am grateful also to my friends Jaques Ferrier and Jean François Drevon for advice and enlightenment. As with every writing I have produced during the last thirty years, I owe much to Liane Lefaivre. Special thanks for friendship and inspiration to Professor F. H. Schroeder, Mercedes Lassus, Micha and Talma Levin, and to my collaborators at Design Knowledge Systems Research Center of TUD Asaf Friedman, Karina Zarzar, and Alkistis Rodi. My greatest debt is to my secretary Janneke Arkenstein, and my student assistants Michael Woodford and Yvonne Modderman for their help and devotion to the project. Many thanks to the Fondation Le Corbusier, Mme. Evelyn Tréhin, to the designers of this book Joseph Cho and Stefanie Lew, and to Terence Maikels, my editor at Universe, for his patience and determination to overcome every difficulty the project encountered.

"To observe is to discover, to invent"   **CHAPTER 01**

Charles-Édouard Jeanneret was born on October 6, 1887, at La Chaux-de-Fonds, Neuchâtel, a small Swiss town on the shore of Lake Neuchâtel, by the slopes of the Chaumont, a thousand meters above sea level, and far from any metropolis. He was the son of Marie-Charlotte-Amélie Jeanneret-Perret, a musician, and Georges-Édouard Jeanneret, a watchmaker and watchcase engraver. At first glance, there appears to be a great contrast between this modest background and the flamboyancy that later marked the funeral of Le Corbusier – the name Charles-Édouard Jeanneret chose as his professional name – which took place in Paris in 1965. Celebrities from all over the world attended the funeral. Indian architects brought water from the Ganges, Greeks, earth from the Acropolis. André Malraux, in a moving farewell on behalf of the French government, informed the crowds that public memorials were being held the same time in Japan and Brazil. It was a proper homage to a man who swayed the design of buildings and cities and revolutionized the way people *see* architecture as no other architect since Palladio.

Repeatedly Le Corbusier used the expression "eyes that do not see" to criticize his contemporaries. By that he stressed that "seeing" is a cognitive rather than a retinal phenomenon. Seeing involves identifying, understanding properties and usages, and follows from learning. Le Corbusier's mission was to instruct his contemporaries how to "see" artifacts rather than to make artifacts just to be seen. Indeed, his structures, paintings, sculptures, and publications were objects *good for learning* and not products to be consumed and experienced only. Le Corbusier changed the world by introducing to it

Le Corbusier with his sculpture *Totem*, Paris, 1961, photographed by Lucien Hervé

his buildings, urban projects, furniture, and art. He also changed it by redesigning our beliefs and desires about it. Just as he made history through his buildings and artifacts, he also wrote his own version of it through the publication of his epic *Œuvre Complète* ("Complete Work"). As with Picasso and Einstein, Le Corbusier had a global impact far beyond the confines of his discipline; he was an architect of *modern life*.

To grasp how Le Corbusier achieved all that and to enjoy more profoundly his masterpieces, it is important to understand how his creative mind worked. Without a doubt he was endowed with a unique ability of visual-spatial thinking; the following text will show how this special gift worked. But he was also endowed with "habits of mind" and "habits of the heart" that sustained his inventive activities. To comprehend them, we have to explore his very early environment. While nobody can claim that his birthplace, La Chaux-de-Fonds, *determined* Le Corbusier's life or work, it did contribute to a way of thinking, without which his achievements would have been impossible.

Much has been written about Nietzsche's heroic image of life, Rousseau's sentiments of nature, and the "machinistic" spirit of the 1920s in Paris that influenced Le Corbusier. Indeed, Le Corbusier was acquainted with their ideas. He had read Nietzsche when he was young, underlining and annotating Nietzsche's texts. He had read Rousseau, and he had studied closely the Parisian avant-garde before becoming part of it. Yet, La Chaux-de-Fonds supplied him with something more fundamental and generic than his later influences. He became acquainted with its past formally through history lessons

Sketch of a shell

and informally through storytelling. These experiences endowed him with what M. Polanyi called a special "tacit knowledge" through which he could grasp unfamiliar conditions and solve crises – he could identify the avant garde and become one of their great protagonists. The avant garde did play a decisive role, equal to that of the contemporary weltanschauung, in the evolution of Charles-Édouard Jeanneret into Le Corbusier.

Le Corbusier himself sketched an accurate history of La Chaux-de-Fonds. He described his ancestors as "French of the South;" they were actually from the Languedoc region. Their ideas were theologically based but were also socialist, reformist, critical, and optimistic. They were against the icons, supported commercial activities, and scrutinized the authority of the church and even the scriptures. Accused as heretics and afraid to be massacred by the "French of the North," the *cathari,* as they were called (meaning "the purists"), escaped to the "rude and stubby" mountains of Neuchâtel in the middle of the fourteenth century. Ever since then, the region has maintained a tradition as an asylum for the persecuted. With the Revocation of the Edict of Nantes, more refugees from France found protection in the mountains of Neuchâtel, whose severe climate and bare soil were not as friendly as their inhabitants. But their rigorous, unyielding, agonistic mentality helped them face this new emergency, survive, and even prosper. Like his ancestors, Le Corbusier throughout his life was consistently optimistic, iconoclastic, and purist. In 1918 he launched a movement under the name *purism* and seven years later he accused the architecture of his time as *iconolatric* and his own position as *iconoclastic.* He was attacked for these ideas but found his persecution stimulating rather than dispiriting and thrived on the public scandal that resulted.

Because the land of La Chaux-de-Fonds was poor, everything had to be produced with great difficulty and risk. The new settlers responded to the conditions by making a rule that everything had to be on time and planned in advance. This rule would become an overriding value in Le Corbusier's theories of architecture and urbanism, together with his loathing of the "bizarre" and the "accidental." Researchers have pointed out that these ideas were the product of the "new spirit" – the industrial, mechanical, scientific spirit of objectivity and precision, solidity and sharpness, law and order of his own times. Le Corbusier became acquainted with this "new spirit" when he settled in Paris. Yet, his values reflected a deeper mentality that he had acquired during his upbringing in La Chaux-de-Fonds, one that has been sustained there for generations.

The La Chaux-de-Fonds immigrants, reflecting upon their arduous lot, realized that there was another option for survival besides working hard on their land to produce basic goods for subsistence: They could import their goods, as long as they could provide something in exchange – in this case, watches. Having brought with them from France the technical knowledge to make a most precious object, these immigrants were ingenious enough to innovate production continuously, revolutionizing the economy of the region. Their success in recruiting the human potential of the region, with their dexterity in needlework, lacework, and jewelry, allowed them to "remake" their skills into the business of watch-making, a product of superior value. Le Corbusier's creative design resulted from his shrewd ability to exercise a kind of cognitive economy, innovating by reinterpreting, reusing, and adapting the resource of existing products.

By the end of the eighteenth century the pattern of migration had reversed, from Neuchâtel to France. Neuchâtelois merchants – with an extraordinary willingness to live abroad – searched for markets rather than shelter. Being on the road was not uncommon for Neuchâtelois. As with Huguenots, Calvinists, and Jews, they moved through the global web of family and personal connections, promoting commerce, finance, and new knowledge. They reached Amsterdam, Marseilles, Constantinople, and even China. Their success led to the eighteenth-century saying "one Genevan is worth six Jews, and one Neuchâtelois, six Genevans." In the nineteenth century, the pioneer designer of the Chevrolet car, Louis Chevrolet, was also born in La Chaux-de-Fonds and went to North America in search of opportunities to implement his design ideas. Le Corbusier followed suit, adopting similar ways of acquiring knowledge, finding clients, and promoting his ideas. "My lot," said Le Corbusier, "is to be an impenitent traveler born into all the corners of the world." Continuing this centuries long practice, and during his travels, he took advantage of the networks of Neuchâtelois, of the Swiss diaspora, and of the avant-garde artists.

La Chaux-de-Fonds faced more crises in its history. Other watchmaking centers, including Geneva, threatened the small town by lowering costs and increasing the quality of their products. Discipline and hard work were not enough to compete. The people of La Chaux-de-Fonds had to redefine their economy and rethink their production as they had when they abandoned agriculture for watchmaking. They had to invent; they succeeded in revolutionizing their production by redefining it as a system, approaching it in a Cartesian way. Thus watchmaking was "reengineered." They analyzed their

Poésie sur Alger, Paris, 1950: book cover

watches and watchmaking, splitting production into elements as well as standardizing modes of production while introducing new forms of division of labor and specialization. Nearly all the city's population, including women and children, participated in the process. Mechanized, power-driven production followed. Soon La Chaux-de-Fonds became "one huge watch manufacturer," as Marx described it in *Das Kapital*, referring to it as an exemplar of early technological systems and rationalized mass production. This improved the marketability of their watches, but it also led to new products, such as watch parts and special-purpose tools. By 1793, La Chaux-de-Fonds exported half a million watch parts. The experience of overcoming crises through invention, Cartesian thinking, and the collaboration of the entire community became part of the collective memory of La Chaux-de-Fonds. This experience formed a cognitive map to navigate through crises. Inherited through history texts and storytelling, it passed from generation to generation. This experience also influenced Le Corbusier in his approach to personal crises, and as will be discussed later, to world crises. He was therefore prepared for contemporary ideas about Taylorization, industrialization, planning, and mass production of housing and how these ideas contribute to survival in what he called "the tough arena of competition."

Throughout its history of migrations and economic crises, La Chaux-de-Fonds continued to be an open community. It attracted numerous Jews who, engaged in commerce, enjoyed the privilege of owning property and who, by the end of the nineteenth century, became influential in town culture by supporting young designers with modern ideas. It was in this protective, porous, and progressive environment that Le Corbusier found his first admirers, commissions, and a successful paradigm of openness and community that he would treasure for the rest of his life.

As a boy, Le Corbusier was one of the poorest students in his class. He appeared distraught, insubordinate, and was always preoccupied with drawing rather than studying. In 1902, at the age of fourteen, two years before he was to finish high school, he instead transferred to a vocational school, the École d'Art, to learn his father's craft, watch engraving. At the École, Le Corbusier's design talent was recognized immediately and he flourished for the next three years. In his fourth year, Le Corbusier abruptly quit watch engraving for architecture, despite his success and his then dislike of architects. Le Corbusier's father feared that his son's future in this field was uncertain. The person who persuaded him to make this move was Charles L'Eplattenier, his instructor and trusted counselor in the École, who, at the words of Le Corbusier, "treated him as a son."

L'Eplattenier was educated in Budapest and Paris and studied art and, to some degree, architecture. A patriotic regionalist, worried of the changes in the watch industry and the limitations of his region, he promoted education in architecture and design in a broader sense for La Chaux-de-Fonds. He recognized Le Corbusier as a zealous, gifted, and enterprising young person. In 1905, he offered Le Corbusier, then an eighteen-year-old student, the opportunity to design the **Villa Fallet**. He continued to instruct Le Corbusier even while L'Eplattenier was traveling abroad, and in 1912, upon Le Corbusier's return from his long trips, he would ask him to teach in the Nouvelle Section de l'École d'Art in La-Chaux-de-Fonds.

Drawing, ca. 1902–1908

Le Corbusier has described his father as a man "of modest origins" who practiced without much success a "foul and loathsome trade ... the making of watch dials," which by 1912 was a declining craft. As opposed to Le Corbusier's supportive mother, who was willing even to serve as a copyist for his manuscripts and provide him with stable support, his father was a rejecting figure. Jeanneret kept a diary, in which he critically recorded his son's deeds together with his own fears and hopes about his son's future. Throughout his youth, Le Corbusier tried to find strong and approving substitutes (like L'Eplattenier) for his repudiating father. At the same time he found pleasure in fighting any disavowing figure, a habit that led, in combination with his regional, inherently adversarial mentality, to his compulsion to invite and celebrate rejection. But, as is clear through their correspondence, Le Corbusier's drive to accomplish resulted also from love, via his desire to fulfill his father's inarticulate, frustrated dreams.

II

Le Corbusier's studies came to completion in 1907. Design rather than construction and technology dominated studies at the École d'Art. John Ruskin's writings and books, which were sympathetic to regionalism, played a major role in his education, as did literature devoted to antiquity and the classical canon. In early autumn of that year, accompanied by his classmate Léon Perrin, he departed for a long educational tour. For sixty-five days they visited northern Italian cities. Often, as in the case of the Byzantine mosaics of Ravenna, art attracted him more than architecture, and Gothic monuments more than Renaissance monuments. He ignored Vicenza and the buildings of Palladio, an architect who, according to some critics, was supposed to have influenced him. Of all sites visited, none moved him

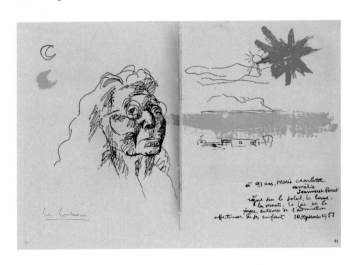

more than the Chartreuse d'Ema in Galluzzo. In a letter to his mentor L'Eplattenier, he called it "heaven upon earth" where he "should like to spend the whole of [his] life ... in what they call ... cells;" it is the solution "to the housing problem." The complex of Ema, he wrote later, reveals the "individual and collectivity as inseparable." His realizations of the building became a significant precedent which he would draw from for the rest of his career.

Le Corbusier's decision to travel was made with the approval of his mentor. The study of monuments and works of art in their own historical setting was part of the normal education of artists or architects during the nineteenth century and the beginnings of the twentieth, if they could afford it. However, the impulsive way Le Corbusier moved around, his spasmodic efforts to combine traveling with employment, and his passionate flight "away from all scholastic instruction ... [feeling] that the work of schools was far removed from reality," resembled Rimbaud's escape rather than an art student's standard tour. He later characterized these traveling years, between October 1907 and October 1917, as a stormy period of his life.

The regular procedure of most young students of this eclectic period, following a rule as old as the Hellenistic times, was to identify and select good parts of historical works, document them, and store them to be reassembled in the future into new perfect wholes. Accordingly, Le Corbusier searched for unfamiliar worlds filled with objects for his thesaurus of precedents to be used when needed in the future. In his short autobiographical text *New World of Space* (1948), he wrote: "everywhere

Drawing of Le Corbusier's mother, ca. 1951, courtesy Fondation Le Corbusier

objects ... are spread before us ... a storehouse of inspiration to draw upon ... have riches to offer which the mind cannot conceive." He collected his material, keeping notebooks and writing numerous letters to his parents and to L'Eplattenier, taking photographs, and buying postcards. Most importantly, he drew. His real tutor, however, was John Ruskin who Le Corbusier believed "knew how to teach one to see." By that, Le Corbusier meant to instruct somebody to find in nature abstract geometrical schemata and rhythmic structures, a lesson that Le Corbusier put into practice. Later, he defined drawing as "observing, discovering ... inventing and creating." Noticeably, invention came after observation. [*Creation is ...*] its function "to push inside the mind" certain objects "inscribed for life." The drawing "is a means to *observe* and in addition to *discover*."

Le Corbusier's next destination was Vienna, where he arrived in November 1907. The city was at that time considered the most important center of architecture, yet Le Corbusier deeply disliked most of its buildings, old and new, the only exception being *Die Fledermaus*, a cabaret designed by Josef Hoffman, the only Viennese architect of whom Le Corbusier approved. Le Corbusier spent considerable time taking drawing lessons, reading, attending the opera or other concerts, and, as he revealed to his parents in a letter, discovering for the first time in his life the deep pleasure of just watching young women. Strangely, a large part of his time in Vienna was spent designing two villas for his hometown, the **Stotzer** and **Jaquemet**. As with Villa Fallet**,** his 1905 project, the influence of L'Eplattenier's regional "Jura" style is obvious. The construction appears naïve but there is sophistication revealed in implanting the building in the site. Even more interesting is the composition of the facades – the shifts

"Eyes that see," sketch from *Le Modulor*, Vol. I (1948), p. 76

between threefold and fourfold rhythms – and of the plans – the tripartite diamond pattern. They reveal an excellent grasp of the classical canon, and they herald his future involvement with it.

As soon as these projects were finished in March 1908, Le Corbusier abandoned Vienna, having stayed there only four months, for Paris. In Paris, he was hired by the great modern architect August Perret and stayed in his office for eighteen months. Perret understood very well Le Corbusier's intentions and allowed him to work part time; Perret soon replaced L'Eplattenier as Le Corbusier's mentor. In contrast to L'Eplattenier, Perret was a construction pioneer who experimented with reinforced concrete but was also a connoisseur of the classical tradition. Under Perret's direction, Le Corbusier tried to catch up with these two major domains of architectural knowledge that he had missed in La Chaux-de-Fonds. He visited Versailles, a place that he later referred to as a precedent for reuse, took history courses at the École des Beaux-Arts, studied at the Bibliothèque Ste. Genevieve, and continued building his own library thanks to his first salary with Viollet-le-Duc Dictionnaire. In Perret's office he was involved in design especially of a Perret villa called Maison Bouteille, following his motto, "a house is a bottle", an analogy Le Corbusier stored also in his thesaurus to reuse several times in the future.

Le Corbusier returned to La Chaux-de-Fonds at the end of 1909, bringing with him the recently published book by E. Mörsch on reinforced concrete, *Le Beton Armé,* given to him by its French translator, the engineer Max du Bois, who was an old classmate of his. He spent the winter of 1910 apart from L'Eplattenier, and was secluded in a farmhouse in the Jura Mountains where his only company

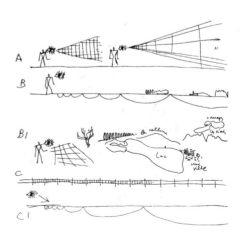

Diagram from *Le Modulor*, Vol. I (1948)

was books on building technology. Reinforced concrete determined to overcome the gaps in his technical education. Soon, however, following once more L'Eplattenier's invitation, he began working on a different subject. The result was his book *La Construction des Villes* ("The Construction of Cities"), for which his mother had served as a copyist assistant. This marked the beginning of his involvement with the pioneering subject of "urbanism." Le Corbusier later would be associated with urbanism as a radical, promoting a rationalist, Cartesian, functional-geometrical approach until the end of his life. However, in 1910, this first essay was conceived under the influences of the picturesque romantic writings of the Viennese Camillo Sitte, L'Eplattenier, and his experiences while visiting medieval sites. He rejected the right angle although he thought it the most beautiful and the rarest in nature. He preferred the line of "least resistance," the zig-zag, that Nature follows and which is exemplified by the route taken by donkeys. (He often suggested, that one should "keep the lesson of the donkey" to achieve effects.) Twelve years later, in 1932, in his project **A Contemporary City for Three Million Inhabitants,** Le Corbusier banished the "donkey route" to confined pockets of the city. The "straight line" took over. Le Corbusier's reasons were that, as opposed to the donkey (i.e., the biological creature), rational man is "walking in a straight line because he has a goal and knows where he is going." Gradually, Le Corbusier found these two ways complementary, first in the small scale of the schemes of his buildings and twenty years later in urbanism, in the scheme for Rio.

In the spring of 1910, Le Corbusier was once more on the road. He briefly visited Munich and moved on to Berlin. In Berlin, he worked full time for another major figure of the modern movement, Peter

Behrens. The job did not allow him to explore Berlin as he had explored Paris. Anyhow, he found Berlin, like Vienna, uninteresting. He spent most of his time there reading books on antiquity, Versailles and Fontainebleau, and the jingoistic writings of Alexandre Cingria-Vaneyre in defense of Greco-Latin classical culture. He also dreamed of escaping to the Mediterranean and did so in May 1911. With German friend and writer August Klipstein, he departed. In the following seven months, they visited the Balkans, Constantinople, Mount Athos, Athens, and Central Italy.

III

Le Corbusier documented his voyage in a series of notebooks published under the title *Voyage d'Orient*. He intended these notebooks for publication, despite his confession that he did not know how to write. In them, there are passages of beauty and happiness but also lines of disgust and anger. He adored Mediterranean nature, buildings, and cities, and he was amused by the chaos of Constantinople – houses, trees, and the space left in between tombs – and the liveliness of courts and cafés. He was overwhelmed by the **Acropolis of Athens** posing "the inexplicable problem": "Why this architecture and no other?" In a text very similar to those of Freud, he described the thoughts of expectation and of "the impossible" to see it as a "dream without even dreaming to realize it, a mad yearning for an unreality." He abhorred tourists – "painful to meet" – as well as the authorities of Stamboul, who sinfully let 9,000 houses burn in a single day while firemen paraded proudly on the other side of the city, and the "narrow patriotism" of the Greeks, whom he described as selling "garbage at scandalous prices."

Sketches from the *Voyage d'Orient:*
view of the Parthenon and the Temple
of Victory (opposite page) and view of
the Propylaea and landscape, Athens,
Greece, 1911 (right)

But the main aim of the *carnets* (notebooks), was to instruct and inscribe in memory, allowing him to teach others and himself how to *see* and how to save precedents in a thesaurus that could be recalled and recombined into new projects for years to come. Text and drawings attach "pointers" and "frames" to the various descriptions of structures and landscapes. Thus, the voyage became a decisive period in his education as an artist and architect.

His drawings in the *Voyage* are very different from those of his previous trip to Italy. They are less dependent on Ruskin, less evocative of memory and atmosphere, and less moody and nostalgic. They teach us to see architecture through the "rectitude of the clear mathematics," as numerical or geometric structures or as "solids and voids," "the play of shadows and light" as "plastic drama." His interest in the tripartite scheme of the classical canon is evident in the documentation of the cases of Byzantine and Ottoman structures. Such instances include the July 1 drawing of the tripartite plan of the **Eksi Djami** of Adrianopole, explicitly marking 3–2–3 and 2–1–2 divisions and the plan for the **Philotheou** monastery in Athos.

The exercise of seeing is extended from autonomous buildings to their relationship with the surrounding landscape. Le Corbusier celebrated the monuments of the Acropolis in harmony with the mountains, the sea, and the sky. He pointed to the "horizontal plane of the highest step" of the Parthenon, "exactly where the columns end, as aligned with the Aegina bay." He recalled this effect when he designed the roof of the **UH** in the late 1940s. In the same building, he also recalls as *pilotis* the effect of the columns

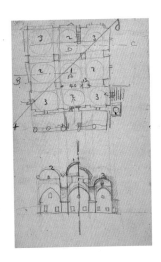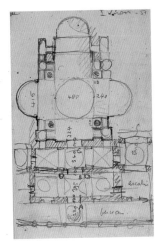

Sketches from the *Voyage d'Orient:*
Filotheou Karyai (left) and Eksi Djami
Adrianoupolis (right)

of the Propylaea, framing the distant view of the **Parthenon**. He was particularly interested in the relation to the sun in certain positions and certain key points of the buildings. In the Parthenon, he identified the straight line linking the sun and the moment it sets, passing between the columns and through
the door with the middle of the dark cella. In another temple, he discovered how the sun "touches the
ground on (the building's) very axis." He even imagined how priests emerging out of the cella of the
Parthenon were sensing "the bosom of the mountains behind them and on their side." He tried to
reproduce this feeling almost half a century later while designing the **Ronchamp**. In a most extravagant
case, he reversed common sense to claim that "the temples (are) the justification of the landscape."

Frequently, seeing goes beyond formal analysis or symbolic interpretations. Striping the ordinary reality of objects allows for powerful visual, surrealist analogies to emerge, giving birth to les *objets à
réaction poétique*. The "strange silhouette;" of the **Cathedral of Estergôn**, formally analyzed as "a
cube and a dome supported by many columns by the rising mountains" is perceived as "an offering
on an altar." Watching "eagles hovering over the geometry of the mosques" he discerns "immense
discs" and reads "the myriad doves surrounding the dome" as a "cloud of wings." Subliminal eroticism,
present throughout the journals, comes onto the surface, giving birth to surrealist carnal images. The
"bronze cannons lying in the sand at the promontory of Seraglio" with their decorated gold rings are
translated into "divine, provoking odalisques" wearing "solid gold rings like serpents around their
naked ankles and arms … their vermilion painted nails." The most powerful and most significant of all
these mental constructs is the Parthenon: "a sovereign cube facing the sea" and "a terrible machine."

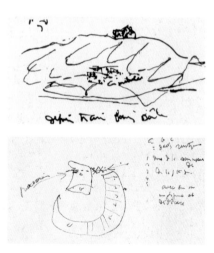

The ruins of the original Chapel at Ronchamp, Carnet Sketchbook 50
Paris-Marseille, 1950 (top); Procession to the Le Corbusier Chapel at
Ronchamp, Carnet Sketchbook E18–Ronchamp, 1950 (bottom)

He brought back the Parthenon machine metaphor as an emblem of the continuity of the pure and the rigorous throughout the high moments of history.

IV

After seven months of traveling, Le Corbusier returned to La Chaux-de-Fonds in November 1911. The next three years were very significant. His long association with L'Eplattenier, which had survived many crises before, came to an end, as did his teaching at the École and his involvement with the regionalist Jura style. "One cannot create a regional architecture intentionally," he wrote. He turned increasingly to the classical canon and to classical examples as well as to precedents from his voyage in the Mediterranean. This is clear in the two villas designed during this period, the **Jeanneret-Perret** for his parents and the **Favre-Jacot** for the founder of the Zenith Watch Company. In the Favre-Jacot, the classical rules are stretched to accommodate the particularities of the site and affirmed through the use of contained anomalies. From the "lively temple with the four faces" – to use Le Corbusier's words describing the Erechthion in his *Voyage* – he recruits the Caryatid portico motif to create a similar "four-faced" building in order to accommodate constraints of the site. Seven years later, Adolf Loos, in collaboration with Paul Engelmann, also tried to use, in a similar manner, the Erechthion, in the Villa Konstandt but with less intriguing results.

Eager to find clients, Le Corbusier became a member of the Nouveau Circle in 1914. The Circle was a notable association founded by members of the Jewish community C F, and was an organization

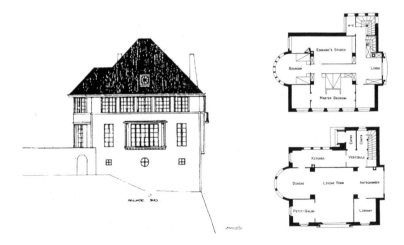

Façade Sud.

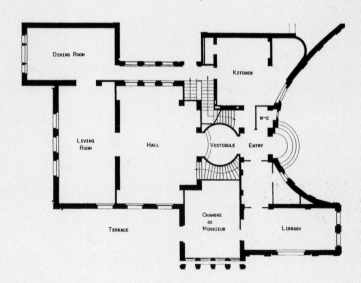

DINING ROOM

KITCHEN

W-C

LIVING ROOM

HALL

VESTIBULE

ENTRY

TERRACE

CHAMBRE DE MONSIEUR

LIBRARY

Villa Jeanneret-Perret: elevation and plans (opposite page); Villa Favre-Jacot: elevation and ground floor plan (above)

Villa Schwob, La Chaux-de-Fonds,
Switzerland, 1916: interior

explicitly open to all faiths that was dedicated to the intellectual, as well as professional, advancement of its members. Le Corbusier's rare personality, combining seriousness and clownish manners; his passion for innovation and knowledge of architecture from books and travels; as well as his enthusiasm and talent charmed and impressed the group. Soon, he received commissions for the interior of the club, for the interiors of the houses of the Ditisheim and Schwob families, and for their offices. Finally, in April 1916, having greatly enchanted Mme. Raphy Schwob and her friend Mme. Ditisheim, (having shown them his parents' house), with Raphy's recommendation he was asked by her cousin Anatole Schwob (1874–1932), executive of Schwob Frères & Co S.A. and the Tavannes Watch Company, to design his house.

Le Corbusier worked on the **Villa Schwob**, specifying the last detail to everything, including giving samples of the tone of the colors to be used. Schwob was happy; however, problems arose as costs mounted during construction. Schwob demanded a new estimate, which turned out to be almost three times the original one. Schwob accused Le Corbusier of deceit. There were counter-arguments, and the case ended in court by a draw with both parties revoking accusations. The dispute became a local legend and the subject of a novel.

The Schwob house was the end of Le Corbusier's line of evolving plans of villas in La Chaux-de-Fonds and the most significant built project before his final move to Paris; it was the bridgehead to a new development. The Schwob house was both the most modern, manifested in the simplification of plans

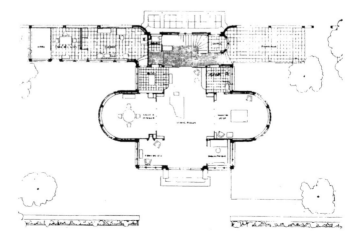

Villa Schwob: ground floor plan

and facades, and the most classical of his projects so far. The latter aspect is clear in the elaboration of the tripartite diamond pattern, which became increasingly vivid as a spatial pattern. In addition, a new theme appeared, that of the unified central double-height space, derived from the Maison Bouteille of Auguste Perret that Le Corbusier later reused in many variations for the rest of his life.

Although Le Corbusier did not include the Villa Schwob in his *Œuvre Complète*, he did give it a prominent place in his manifesto *Vers une Architecture*. It appears next to the Petit Trianon and the Capitol of Rome as a good example of *regulating lines*, using geometry as a means to install "order" and avoid "capriciousness" in the human world, another principle he followed throughout all his projects. As opposed to Villa Schwob, **les Maisons Dom-ino** project, designed almost at the same time, is included in the *Œuvre Complète*, and justifiably so. In stark contrast with Villa Schwob, Dom-ino was a building type of a construction-production system and concerned the greater number.

It is remarkable that in 1913 Le Corbusier, in the midst of designing villas and luxury interiors, was also busy establishing his own office. His intention was to specialize in reinforced-concrete construction with the intention of nothing less than revolutionizing the management and production of housing. Even more note worthy was that most of his thinking was carried out in collaboration with his old friend, the engineer Max du Bois, who was in Paris. Le Corbusier sketched for him the idea of a new spatial and construction system beginning that year. It was the first outline of Les Maisons Dom-ino. The outbreak of World War I in August 1914 gave Le Corbusier a sense of urgency. To overcome the crisis he

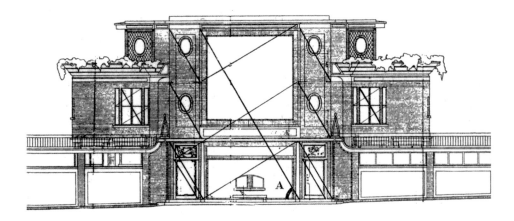

searched for a solution in technological innovation. Being Swiss and, because of his health, not being in the reserve, Le Corbusier was not affected directly by the war. The news of the devastation, however, had a major impact on his thinking. Despite the war, by the summer of 1915, he was back in Paris for a meeting with Max du Bois to discuss the project. Finally the **emblematic schema** that crystallized the idea was drawn late in 1915.

The Dom-ino project consists of a rectangular "skeleton" scheme and a number of plans and perspectives showing a variety of units and site arrangements. The frame is made out of reinforced concrete: six columns of standardized size, slightly raised from the ground on six footings that support floor slabs and stairs. The floor slabs are smooth, without beams supporting them. The columns are on the perimeter of the structure but do not reach the edge of the floors. Thus, facades, walls, fenestration, and doors are independent of the structure. The project encompassed aspects of management, construction, and design. It was conceived as a universal prototype system for putting together any kind of building that responded to the colossal postwar needs while at the same time exploiting the vast opportunities offered by new means of construction and industrial production.

Maisons Dom-ino appeared as a purely formal technical project. As such, it owed much to E. Mörsch's monolithic reinforced concrete construction and to François Hennébique's concrete frame. On the other hand, Maisons Dom-ino is more than a formal technical schema; it is an intellectual construct standing for more general principles and values that Le Corbusier created by erecting it on deeper

Villa Schwob: elevation (left);
Dom-Ino system 1913 (right)

historical foundations. These principles can be traced to the Enlightenment's architectural rigorist movement, as expressed in Abbé Laugier's skeleton of the primitive hut made out of essential parts only. But they can be identified better if one digs deeper in time. The minimal scheme of the Dom-ino manifests a clearly cathartic iconoclastic stance, opposing, in the words of Le Corbusier, the "acceptance of forms, methods, concepts because they exist, without asking why … without involving his own self in every question." He noted: "Conventions, customs are words of surrender." Having refused their "state of slavery," Le Corbusier proceeded by splitting the traditional building fabric into "elementary atoms." There is revealed the La Chaux-de-Fonds operation of radical division of labor and redistribution of the parts of the building, but also a Cartesian judgment to define only those things about which one is certain.

The way Le Corbusier proceeded creating the Dom-ino is elucidated, referring to the 1930 text and diagrams of *Précisions*. Traditional concepts were considered "paralyzing," "wasteful," "parasitic," and "anachronistic." He got rid of them. Thus, masonry walls were analyzed into the operations of support and separation and replaced by two "pure" elements: columns and "partitions," or rather *"diaphragms,"* exterior or interior. With them go the traditional notions of "room" and "corridor" replaced by "function" and the "organ of horizontal circulation" and "furniture" by "equipment." There is no more "back" or "front" of the building. Conceptual purification and analysis brings a new freedom: the "free plan," the "free facade," and the freedom to make infinite combinations of the unit. "We are now tooled to find solutions for the … modern house." Suddenly, "everything was possible." "Light, air," and "vegetation" "go through," they "flow under the house." There is the new opportunity to have a "garden on

Aqueduct, *Sketchbook* A1, Landeron,
9, Fondation Le Corbusier

the roof" and a "horizontal window" offering undisturbed views and an infinite number of combinations of interior partitions. Last, but not least, this new "purified" and redefined type of building permits standardization and subsequently industrialization and mass production.

"Today I am considered a revolutionary," declared Le Corbusier in *Précisions*. There is no doubt that Dom-ino was a revolutionary project in the same way that the ideas of Gottlob Frege, Bertrand Russell, and the analytical philosophers who were contemporaries of Le Corbusier, undertook a similar task to purify and recast language. All were revolutionary, ultimately revolutionizing more industrialization rather than distribution of power. Unlike these philosophers, however, Le Corbusier and his revolution were very much utilizing historical precedent rather than drawing on a tabula rasa. One could claim that the form of the Dom-ino scheme was recruited from the minimal skeleton and flat roof of the Acropolis structures as sketched by Le Corbusier during his *Voyage*. Le Corbusier himself suggested that his "revolutionary ideas are *in* history, in every period and every country."

The idea of the Dom-ino became the theoretical basis of most of his houses up to 1935 and was extended on a scale much beyond the two-story house. Combined with Eugène Hénard's idea of Rue Future, it led to the Ville Pilotis, the city on piles, as well as to a number of prototype buildings such as the Unité d'Habitation. In January 1917, Le Corbusier, with the idea of the Dom-ino still a promise and the troubles of Villa Schwob still unsettled, said farewell to La Chaux-de-Fonds and settled permanently in Paris.

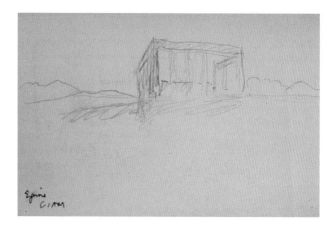

Temple of Aegina, 1933, *Sketchbook*
B5, p. 312, Fondation Le Corbusier

"Forging the tools of an epoch"   **CHAPTER 02**

I

Le Corbusier moved to Paris in 1917 with almost no money and very few contacts. Intellectually, however, he was ready to face the challenge. He had a reserve of projects and he was waiting to find the opportunity to materialize a wealth of accumulated knowledge and to go about implementing them. His faithful old friend and recent collaborator, Max du Bois, who already was both socially and professionally established in Paris, introduced him immediately to engineers, industrialists, bankers, and potential clients. Many of them were Swiss, such as Raoul La Roche, a Basel banker and the director of the Crédit Commercial de France. Du Bois set up for Le Corbusier a network of organizations involved in the construction and manufacturing of building products. Continuing his ideas that were developed before in the Dom-ino project but also responding to new challenges posed by Tony Garnier's *La Cité Industrielle*, which was published the year of his arrival in Paris, Le Corbusier tried to reform building production, even launching in 1919 a factory that produced concrete blocks. With the same enthusiasm that he had immersed into this half-technical, half-entrepreneurial world, he plunged into serious painting, seeing no conflict between the two fields. Three years later the concrete block enterprise closed down. Nothing would deter Le Corbusier from continuing to develop new construction components, trying new materials, and even seeking patents while at the same time painting systematically and having an active social life.

At the end of his first year in Paris, during a lunch at the Art et Libertè, August Perret introduced him to Amédée Ozenfant. Ozenfant, the son of a licensee contractor of the reinforced concrete pioneer,

Hennébique, was only one year older than Le Corbusier and was already an established avant-garde artist. He was known for his journal *l'Élan*, which he founded in 1915 with Guillaume Apollinaire and Max Jacob.

An intimate, intense, and highly productive intellectual relationship began between Le Corbusier and Ozenfant. As with Le Corbusier's previous friendships, however, it did not last long, this time for only five years. During this period, Le Corbusier and Ozenfant shared a studio, painted, and exhibited together. In collaboration with the poet Paul Dermée and with financial support and advice from La Roche, they launched in 1920 a new journal, *L'Esprit Nouveau* ("The New Spirit"). It was a unique, multidisciplinary, cultural publication devoted to modern art, literature, music (Albert Jeanneret, Le Corbusier's brother, was a musician who wrote on music), and architecture. It was in this journal that Charles-Édouard Jeanneret's nom de plume, Le Corbusier, appeared for the first time. The publication was read and emulated around the world.

The most significant product of Ozenfant's and Le Corbusier's collaboration was writing *Après le Cubisme* ("After Cubism"), a book that was released in November 1918 and that launched a new movement, *purism*. Their aim was to move modern art beyond a state of "decadence," for which they considered cubism responsible. Quoting Voltaire in the opening of the book, they claimed that cubism led to a condition, in which "making things was too easy and a laziness in making them well, a saturation of beauty and an inclination towards the bizarre." They called their movement *purism*, indicating an approach that led art and architecture away from decadence by stripping away and purging the "accidental" and the "impressionistic" and expressing the "constants." Their two suggestions as to where to find these constants were both "Kantian" and "Hegelian." The Kantian suggestion called for a return to an a priori order of human nature; the Hegelian, for catching up with the spirit of the new order of the epoch that produced industrial buildings, engineering structures, and machines "as projections of the laws of nature." Although so different, both approaches led to the same prescription: an art of "pure form" that cubism, as well as other decadent practices in action at that time, destroyed through "decoration" or "camouflage." They asked for an art of elementary geometrical forms derived from "calculation," which organized through number geometrical "grids" and "ordering axes" – what would later become in Le Corbusier's vocabulary "regulating lines" – "a painting is nothing but an equation"; together with architecture it expresses "fundamental principles."

The book situated Le Corbusier within the art debate of his time. But it was more than a manifesto of purism as a formal idiom but also of purism as an intellectual, moral stance, a "purist" way of thinking and a way of living. Interestingly, the name of the movement, *purism,* is a translation of *cathares*, the name given to Le Corbusier's Languedoc ancestors – *cathares* in Greek, means "*pure*." But the basic conceptual framework of the argument also revealed deep affinities with the mentality of those iconoclastic

Maison Citrohan: 1922 version

"heretics" and their vision of good life. The link became more explicit in 1925, the year Le Corbusier broke with Ozenfant, in his *L'Art décoratif d'aujourd'hui* ("Decorative Arts of Today"). In the book, which focused on interiors and furniture, Le Corbusier mapped the contemporary artistic cultural situation divided between two camps, the "iconolaters" and the "iconoclasts." The latter was a view held by the *cathari*. Linking his contemporary epoch with a centuries-long conflict, Le Corbusier explicitly identified himself as siding with the iconoclasts, those who "protest" "in the name of everything" including "morality" and "our ancestors whose labor makes us respect them" and those who consider culture a "path towards internal life."

In a cross-cultural, cross-historical leap, however, he included Lenin among the iconoclasts, sipping coffee from a small white cup, sitting on a tube chair, wearing a bowler hat, and surrounded by other quotidian, mass-produced, purist paraphernalia. This was a typical Le Corbusier analogical leap. A similar analogical leap had already been made in his famous Parthenon–1921 Grand-Sport automobile analogy in *Vers une architecture nouvelle* ("Toward a New Architecture"), a book Le Corbusier originally published in 1923 that revamped a series of articles he had contributed together with Ozenfant in *L'Esprit nouveau*. The book revealed Le Corbusier's compulsory mental fabrication of associations with tremendous rhetorical, creative, and instructive power – making people "see" the world in a new way. At the same time it manifested his deep belief in the universality of human cultures and history.

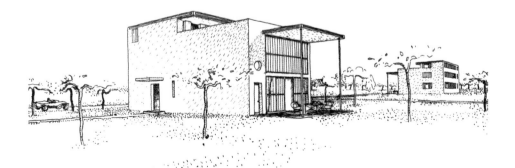

II

As with many Parisian artists and intellectuals of this period, Le Corbusier and Ozenfant carried out their intense collaborations in the unpretentious Café Mauroy. Its pure, compact interior volume, split by a mezzanine, became one of the precedent-types in Le Corbusier's thesaurus of spatial schemes. It was first applied in 1920 with the **Maison Citrohan** in Beaulieu-sur-mer. As with all the projects until the end of their partnership, Maison Citrohan was designed in collaboration with his cousin Pierre Jeanneret. Citrohan, like Dom-ino, was not realized, but within Le Corbusier's architectural life it is a seminal project. Le Corbusier conceived it as a prototype for mass-housing – thus the name Citroën intended to be associated with the famous mass-produced French car. The scheme, a "true" "pure prism," consisted of a minimal structure of two parallel bearing walls, the mezzanine floor, and a flat roof that was turned into a *roof garden*. In its 1922 version, the prism was raised on *pilotis*, introducing a new element in Le Corbusier's toolbox. An application of the prototype was tried for the city of Stuttgart for the **Colony of Weissenhof Development** in 1927.

Villa for the Weissenhof Development, Stuttgart, Germany, 1927

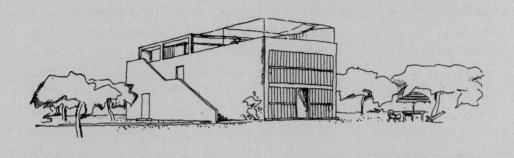

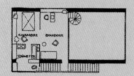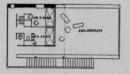

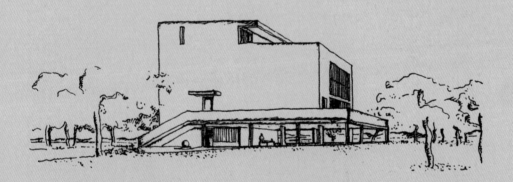

Maison Citrohan, 1920 version (top); Maison Citrohan, 1920 version: ground floor, mezzanine, and roof terrace plans (middle); Maison Citrohan, 1922 version (bottom)

In addition to mass housing, Le Corbusier carried on with the application of the precedent of the Café Mauroy mezzanine and the principles of purism to buildings of exceptional lifestyles, such as the **house and studio for Ozenfant** in Paris. This project was designed in 1922, the year Le Corbusier entered into practice with his cousin Pierre Jeanneret, a partnership that lasted until the outbreak of World War II. The scheme drew from the Maison Citrohan precedent. Following the classical rule of deformation for adapting a type into a site, a Serlio rule known to Le Corbusier from his French classical literature sources, the Citrohan double-square plan was deformed to adapt to the specific constraints of the site. The front and back openings were varied to accommodate light and viewing needs, and one of the side walls was opened to introduce necessary light. Despite these irregularities, Le Corbusier promised for order to reign. Indeed, one finds an aura of completeness and coherence emerging from the project. It follows from the "command," in the words of Le Corbusier from *L'Art décoratif*, echoing the *cathari* spirit, "love purity." It comes forth following the principle, "no dirty corner, no dark corner," applying what he called the "moral law of *ripolin*" – painting with white enamel the whole building. Metaphorically, the product was purified through the use of *regulatory lines* that purged the "false," bringing about agreement in the composition. Le Corbusier promised that the building would be rich in its bareness, "whitewash" being the richness of "the poor and the rich" and of "the slave and the king" and happy in its strictness with the elimination of the "non-essential" leading to the "joy of life."

Le Corbusier and Pierre Jeanneret: Atelier Ozenfant, Paris, France, 1922, courtesy Fondation Le Corbusier

Le Corbusier and Pierre Jeanneret:
Atelier Ozenfant: view of studio,
courtesy Fondation Le Corbusier

The same year Le Corbusier designed his first villa in Paris, the **Villa Besnus at Vaucresson** for M. Georges Besnus. In this minimal project, Le Corbusier introduced three significant new design principles. Within the framework of division of labor and specialization, he split the vertical circulation "service-organ" from the volume of the residence it serves and removed it outside, attaching one next to the other. This was an idea developed already within the tradition of French classical architecture by the Renaissance architect Du Cerceau. Le Corbusier later followed this principle in most of his projects, irrespective of scale. He also worked out the principle of the horizontal window, consequent to the independence of the exterior walls from the structure. This new kind of opening offered a panoramic spectacle of the landscape, an effect that Le Corbusier had already observed in his *Voyage*, in Balkan and Istanbul houses, and noted down even on a boat traveling in Lake Léman in Switzerland. Last but not least, the Villa Besnus offered him the opportunity to inquire into the possibilities of a purist composition in harmony with the classical canon. Both plan and facade are based on a strict tripartite scheme. However, the scheme uses classical, subtle, rhetorical figures of contained anomalies. There is a contradiction between placing a stressed element in the middle of the two side parts and a nonstressed element in the center of the whole – a figure employed in the **Porte Saint-Denis** by François Blondel that Le Corbusier reproduced in *Vers une architecture*. Rather than subverting it, the paradox enables the understanding of order as worked out through centuries by the classical canon.

Le Corbusier and Pierre Jeanneret:
Atelier Ozenfant: view of studio,
courtesy Fondation Le Corbusier

Le Corbusier and Pierre Jeanneret:
Maison La Roche, Paris, France, 1923,
courtesy Fondation Le Corbusier

More idiosyncratic than the studio was the **Villa La Roche** for his friend, the banker Raoul la Roche. Located in 10, Square du Docteur-Blanche, the exclusive sixteenth arrondissement in Paris; this was one of the happiest projects for Le Corbusier. Commissioned in 1923 and designed during 1924, the villa came to realization in 1925. Initially, Le Corbusier tried to develop the whole street on which the site was located. The undertaking was not different from that of Robert Mallet-Stevens just a block away. Le Corbusier acted as real estate broker, negotiating with landowners, bankers, and potential clients, including Lotti Raaf-Walberg, his brother's wife, who immediately commissioned him to build a house for her and her husband, Albert. In contrast to La Roche's house for a bachelor, and a rich art collector, the **Villa Jeanneret-Raaf** was for a family of relatively modest means. Space is divided according to the traditional concept of "corridors" and "rooms," compact as in the standard Maison Citrohan. As with that project, there is a roof garden that becomes even more important because it includes the kitchen and the dining place, which are situated away from the street, "towards the light and the *pure* air."

In his *Œuvre,* Le Corbusier points out that through these two projects he addressed a generic problem in search of a prototypical solution. He tried to develop an urban scheme that could accommodate two houses for two radically different clients with radically different everyday activities into a single synthesis. Despite this difference, the clients of 10, Square du Docteur-Blanche shared a common background and mentality – as did later clients of a series of villas in Paris that follow the Docteur-Blanche project. These clients were foreigners living in Paris. Together with a group of other young

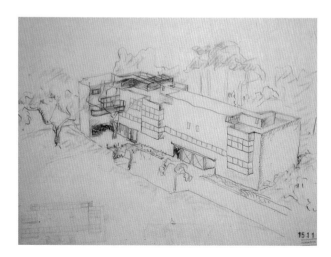

Le Corbusier and Pierre Jeanneret:
Maison La Roche: preliminary sketch

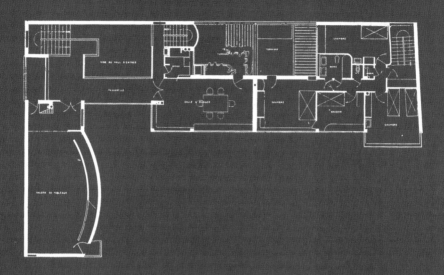

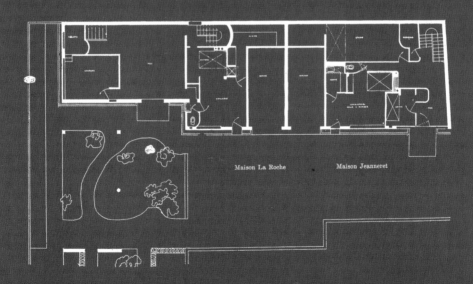

Maison La Roche   Maison Jeanneret

entrepreneurs, artists, intellectuals, and foreign and French professionals, they were part of the same postwar generation eager to take over not so much their own countries – the idea of a nation did not appeal to them as it did the rest of the world. They saw themselves as elite and aspired to use the new potentials of science, industry, and organization to overcome the old parochialism, superstitions, and the elements of conservatism. They experimented with new ways of living and new forms of relating to each other. In this respect Le Corbusier felt that women in particular, referring to 1920s-era feminism "have preceded us [men]," as he remarks in 1930 in *Precisions*. Their "courage, the liveliness, the spirit of invention with which they have operated … are a miracle of modern times." The young women and men of this group craved the opportunities for leadership opened by the collapse of traditional institutions, values, and beliefs, yet they did not aspire to a political movement. They sought a symbolic but concrete demonstration of the new world they desired and a symbolic but physical manifestation of their identity as a group. Le Corbusier, in his 10, Square du Docteur-Blanche project, with its overall compositional unity, purism of content, and newness, appears to have provided a microcosm of the world they desired. Yet, Villa la Roche and the villas of the 1920s that followed, commissioned by these liberal-thinking people, were not tailored to satisfy only the specific agenda of a small group of clients. Le Corbusier was running through his mind many programs in parallel, intending many tasks at the same time. Among them was "patient research," which tried to remake the world according to his own desires and beliefs, both moral and formal.

Le Corbusier and Pierre Jeanneret: Maison La Roche: ground floor plan (opposite page, bottom) and first floor plan (opposite page, top); view of the gallery (right), courtesy Fondation Le Corbusier

Today one admires the L-shaped open configuration of the two villas in 10, Square du Docteur-Blanche, as they are surrounded by gardens. As it stands, however, the composition is incomplete. Villa La Roche together with a villa for S. Marcel, which was never built, formed a neoclassical penta-partite composition. This composition resembles a series of investigations that Le Corbusier carried out during the same period in his paintings, manifesting on one hand the desire to conquer new, unexplored spatial-formal structures and on the other a return to Poussin and compliance with the classical canon. The same duality applies to the interior of the villa.

One enters in a triple-height hall from which the various parts of the building flow out – a theme that owes much to Maison Bouteille. As one would expect in any house, it was divided into public and private zones. However, the plan is dominated by protruding stairs, landings, a ramp, and a bridge, interpenetrating elements of circulation rather than traditional corridors. This arose from the client's need to display his collection of paintings, which included Picasso, Gris, Braque, as well as Ozenfant and Le Corbusier. In his last interview, in 1965, Le Corbusier remembered telling La Roche, "I am going to make for you one hell of an architectural promenade." This is how he created what he called the *promenade architecturale,* a path through and around spaces and volumes of the building designed with the aim to offer an aesthetic experience. But it also followed from Le Corbusier's beliefs that circulation is as important as structure – "architecture is circulation" and it ought to be properly articulated.

Le Corbusier and Pierre Jeanneret: Maison La Roche: gallery and mezzanine, courtesy Fondation Le Corbusier

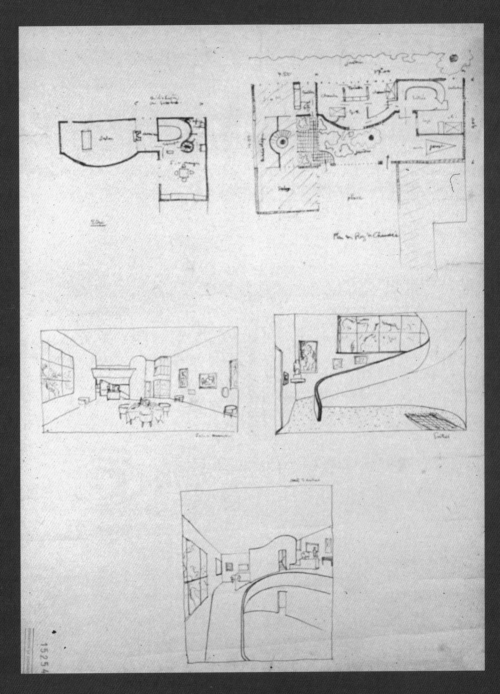

Looking at the plan of the project, in embedding movement within it, Le Corbusier fused his afore-mentioned two approaches to circulation: the "donkey's zigzagging route" and the targeted "straight line." He assigned the first "where one knows where one is going": in the interior of the individual units for sleeping, studying, and cooking. And, having learned the "lesson of the donkey," the second approach was applied from the entrance to the library to the roof/secret garden, for wandering and gazing at the paintings. While one could easily trace the idea of the *promenade* to the French version of the picturesque garden, with which Le Corbusier was very familiar, it is very obvious that Le Corbusier developed the new concept and used as a precedent the palindromic procession in the Acropolis. Le Corbusier recorded the Acropolis in his 1911 *Voyages*; he had read about it in books by architecture historian and archeologist François Auguste Choisy and had reproduced its illustration in *Vers une architecture,* which Le Corbusier published that year.

Despite the overt presence of so many aspects of movement, the space strangely appears serene and poised. This is because, while the interior is organized for movement, its partitioning, which dictates how the elements are placed within it (including those dedicated to movement), applies a classical tri-partite schemata of space division and the informality of the *promenade architecturale*, only to enhance the presence of the classical canon. Nonetheless, responding to the challenge to create a new, open architecture, the building does not sit on a podium, nor does it end on a cornice. There is no distinc-tion between top and bottom, no accentuated terminating corners, and no hierarchy of the various architectural elements.

Le Corbusier and Pierre Jeanneret: Maison La Roche: preliminary sketches, 1923

The same applies to the color. Colors were applied with a carefully chosen palette for few chosen elements to heighten the whiteness of the whole. As a result one has the feeling that Le Corbusier's purist principle, "no dirty corner, no dark corner," the "law of *ripolin*" (white enamel paint), was slavishly obeyed, to produce spaces of "chalky milky" quality.

Another classical figure, through which unity in the composition was achieved, was through the use of *regulatory lines* for the facade. Le Corbusier already employed it for the Villa Schwob. The Villas Schwob and La Roche, together with Ozenfant's studio and the preceding Porte Saint-Denis by François Blondel, were used as examples of the use of regulatory lines in *Vers une architecture*.

La Roche had given complete license to Le Corbusier to apply his ideas expecting that he would make "an object of great beauty." The villa was indeed a success. Architects admired it and La Roche felt that his "hopes were fulfilled." "This house gives me a great joy and I would like to express you my gratitude for that," said La Roche to Le Corbusier when the villa was finished. To demonstrate his satisfaction, he offered a small car as a present to him. La Roche enjoyed living in his villa until 1963, despite its many technical deficiencies, such as a noisy central heating system that was never resolved and despite an ever-pending lighting solution. He found great delight in the various innovations of the house and he was confident that it was an epochal work. In an interview before his death, La Roche admitted how proud he was that Le Corbusier considered the villa a critical moment in the evolution

Le Corbusier and Pierre Jeanneret:
Maison La Roche: roof terrace

of his work, "a point of departure." Today, the building houses the headquarters of the Fondation Le Corbusier.

III

Throughout the 1920s, Le Corbusier designed a series of villas with the rigor of a mathematician who, having set out definitions and principles, produces new propositions and theorems, or the system of a musician composer who, having established a theme and rules, moves on composing variations. Indeed, as much as the 1920s-era projects appear to respond to the specifics of each client and site, they do evolve out of a logic of their own and in relation to each other, experimenting with possibilities of spatial composition.

The **Villa Meyer**, in Paris (designed in 1925, the year Villa La Roche was constructed), remained a project on paper and was known through a much-reproduced letter by Le Corbusier to his client Madame Lise Meyer-Migaud. In this most significant document, Le Corbusier, through the comic-strip technique of words interlocked with magnificent sketches, delineated the basic principles of the design and their spatial counterpart in the future project. In the version presented here, the ground floor is enclosed and the main vertical circulation is taken out of the prismatic volume of the building – a theme Le Corbusier had first discovered three years before in the Villa Besnus in 1923. Following the purist principle, the "laws" of movement determined the curved form of this "organ" of circulation. In

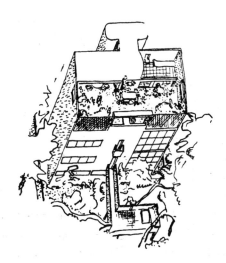

Le Corbusier and Pierre Jeanneret:
Villa Meyer, Paris, France, 1925

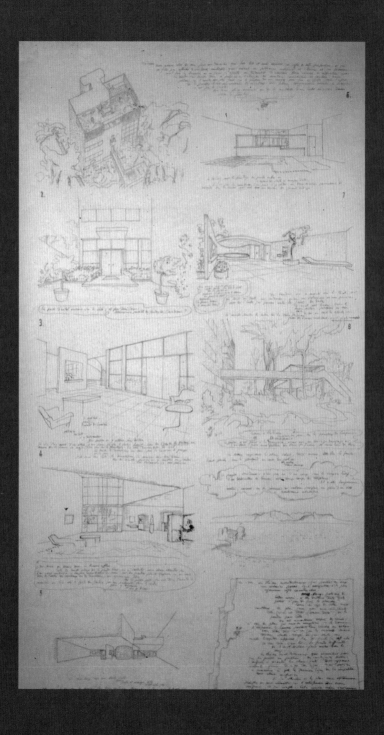

an earlier version of Villa Meyer, Le Corbusier tried another combination. He raised the volume on *pilotis* and contained the vertical circulation inside the prismatic orthogonal cage of the reinforced concrete structure, "like an organ" contained inside a skeleton.

In the letter to Madame Meyer, Le Corbusier was eager to demonstrate the interaction between the openness of the "plan libre" and the sequences of *promenade architectural*. In drawings resembling film pioneer Sergei Eisenstein's scenario sketches, he gave a virtual tour of the future project through a montage of juxtaposed step-by-step, "shot"-by-"shot," short-long vistas. Within each drawing, to use Eisenstein's phrase, "the line is the trail of movement," intended to represent how one captures built space while moving.

The **Villa Cook** in Bologne-sur-Seine in Paris, for the American journalist William Cook, followed the year after Meyer and was more lucky. Commissioned in April 1926, it was realized by March 1927. The structure combines the *pilotis* with bearing wall schema and the idea of leaving the ground floor free. The "organ of circulation" is contained within the prismatic limits of the volume. The absence of a solid base; the horizontal element that frames the volume of the roof garden, without stressing the termination; the pentapartite division of the facade, unified by the horizontal windows and syncopated by the protruding balcony all imply the aura of the classical canon without disclosing it. In the **Villa d'Avray** or **Church** (commissioned in 1927 and finished in 1929), for Mr. and Mrs. Henry Church, who were also American, a similar strategy of local violations and global affirmation of the tripartite/

Le Corbusier and Pierre Jeanneret: Villa Meyer, Paris, France, 1925

pentapartite schema of the classical canon is pursued. There is no *pilotis*, but the roof garden is one of the most developed in this series. This villa was remarkably provided by the Charlotte Perriand-Le Corbusier *equipement*, the new term Le Corbusier introduced in his campaign to "purify" language, to think and talk afresh about "furniture." Perriand, during Le Corbusier's office in 1922 and with several interruptions remained his design partner, but not associate, until the beginning of the 1950s.

Even more excessive use of these devices was made in the **Villa Stein de Monzie**, which is also known as ***Les Terrasses*** or ***Garches.*** It was commissioned in 1925 and completed in 1928. The clients were two Americans: Michael and Sarah Stein (Michael was the brother of the modernist writer Gertrude Stein, who was herself a major collector of paintings by modernists such as Picasso and Matisse) and Madame Gabrielle de Monzie, a friend of the couple and the former wife of Minister Anatole de Monzie. More than Villa Church, the scheme is a catalogue of classical subtle rhetorical figures of contained anomalies and prepared paradoxes. In superposing patterns, there is a systematic shift between stressing and nonstressing the center – a figure employed in the Porte Saint-Denis by Francois Blondel that Le Corbusier reproduced in *Vers une architecture*. Superimposed parts overlap. And behind the apparently open, almost Mondrian-like composition of the facade, which is made out of horizontal window stripes, a classical tripartite/pentapartite schema affirms the order of the classical canon. The project has been called Palladian. However, it is more obvious that Le Corbusier, who totally ignored Palladio during his visit to Italy, drew from precedents of French classical architecture and its rules, which he knew in depth.

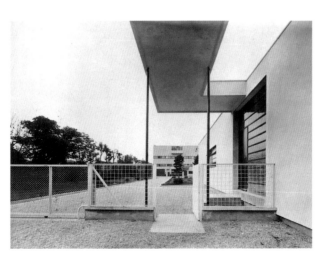

Le Corbusier and Pierre Jeanneret:
Villa Stein de Monzie, Garches, France
1928 (above and opposite page), both
courtesy Lucien Herve

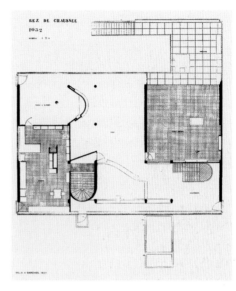

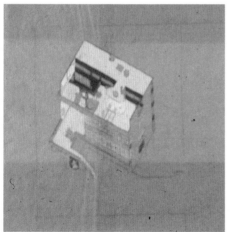

Le Corbusier and Pierre Jeanneret: Villa Stein de Monzie: conceptual sketches (opposite page);
axonometric views and first floor plan (above)

The characterization "Palladian" is perhaps more suitable for **Villa Savoye** in Poissy (Yvelines), which was commissioned by Pierre Savoye for his wife and their son. Like the Villa Rotonda, the building is a kind of belvedere, with views commanding an orchard, or, to be close to the Le Corbusier spirit, a *machine for making "eyes see"* the landscape. The plan is almost square, and a tripartite structure divides the volume both horizontally and vertically. The ground level is a loggia-pilotis around the "organ" of circulation, shaped by the movement of the turning car that parks under the building. The middle level is occupied by a *piano nobile*. A horizontal window runs across the three sides of the floor, framing the landscape in a panoramic manner. More than in any other project this theme was applied before by Le Corbusier. It shows its effect in intensifying the outline of the objects in the horizon and foregrounding the profile of the skyline. Making "eyes see" the landscape is enhanced by the *promenade architectural*. Palindromic ramps cut vertically the volume of the whole villa, enabling the viewers to construct and juxtapose in their minds slices of diametrically opposed prospects. The building terminates in a roof-garden solarium, again a device to make people "see the landscape." As with environmental art today, the roof structures, running, turning, enclosing, and opening walls, columns, and roofs, provide a variety of built edges, bases, and frames that point and focus, evoke and anticipate, offering multiple new interpretations of the landscape to the visitor.

Commissioned in 1928 and completed in 1931, the villa had an unhappy life. It was never meant to be a "quotidian functional" building; rather, as with the Villa Rotonda, it was intended by Le Corbusier to be "poetry produced by technology" for people who were to spend their weekends, "inserted in a

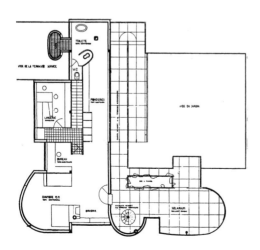

Le Corbusier and Pierre Jeanneret:
Villa Savoye, Poissy, France, 1929
(above), photograph by Michael Levin;
plan of roof garden (opposite page)

Virgilian dream," as he put it. However, as usual, Le Corbusier carried out experiments with risky, untested technology, and here he was not lucky. The building turned into an environmental and technical nightmare.

His total irresponsibility in relation to the clients of Villa Savoye, who were very close friends, was not very different from the fiasco he created by designing in the mountains an architecturally interesting but highly inappropriate house for his parents in Switzerland. Like Madame Savoye, they did not have the chance to enjoy their building, but for different reasons. Their house was beyond their economic and physical means and they were obliged to abandon it. However, they entrusted their son once more to build a **petite villa** on **Lake Léman** near Vevey for their retirement in 1925. Like the Villa Savoye, this small, horizontal structure, built five years before, is a *machine to make "eyes see."* All spaces, with the exception of the kitchen, are paraded in succession, facing the water via a long window running across the façade, thus framing the Mediterranean-like profile of the mountains across the lake. In a fascinating oxymoronic move, Le Corbusier decided to block part of the marvelous distant view by raising a wall, only to revert his decision by opening a window in it. The result achieved was what contemporary poetics would have called a rich *defamiliarization* effect, making common things appear strange and fresh, worth all the devices employed in the machinery of the Villa Savoye. Unlike the Villa Savoye and more like the Villa La Roche, in the house Le Corbusier built for his parents, architect and client appeared in perfect dialogue.

Le Corbusier and Pierre Jeanneret: Villa Savoye: terrace (opposite page) and interior ramp (right), both photographs by Michael Levin

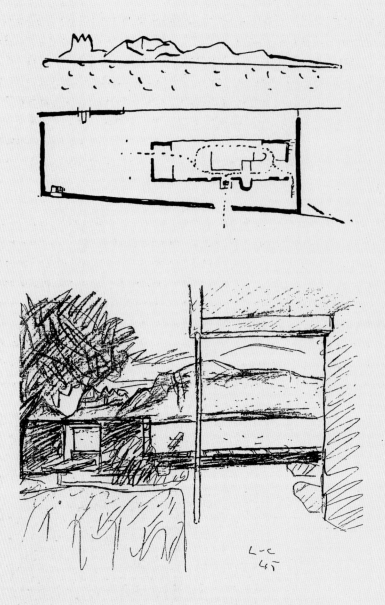

Parents' house, Lake Léman, 1925 (opposite page, courtesy
Fondation Le Corbusier): site plan and landscape sketches (above)

IV

The scheme for Ozenfant's studio served as an experiment to explore the possibility of combining the home and workplace. The basic idea of the loft was carried over two years later in the 1924 project for a series of **mass-produced artisans' dwellings**. Probably inspired by the oblique shape of the Ozenfant site, Le Corbusier introduced for these projects a diagonal line offering a longer dimension in the volume and a loft area covering half of the total. He reused the loft idea again in a 1925 project for **student housing**. In both schemes the precedent of the monastery of Ema was employed, splitting the private realm of the residences from the communal facilities. The scheme of the loft would remain a standard theme for Le Corbusier, but only for his residential buildings. The workplace was not very much the subject of his later inquiries.

While busy designing exclusive avant-garde villa projects, Le Corbusier did not stop investigating the question of mass-produced social housing. Not only did he not find any contradiction being involved in two such diverse domains (between upper- and lower-class housing), he saw both as being variants of the same world. In the purist framework, there was no high or low culture or open-ended progress, there were only cycles of advancement and decadence. As stated earlier, Le Corbusier was involved in parallel programs, each reinforcing the other. He tried to use the opportunity of working with one to develop schemes that could be reused for the other. His thesaurus of possibilities drew from historical monuments as well as humble popular architecture and spaces designed by engineers, such as boat cabins or train compartments, to be reused without any discrimination in villas or social housing alike.

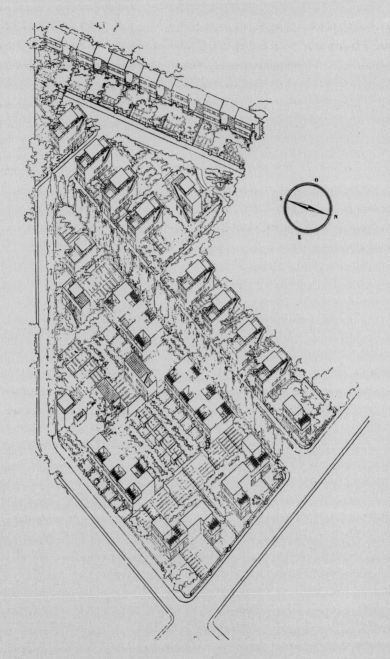

Cité-Jardin Frugès, Pessac-Bordeaux, 1924–1926: axonometric drawing (above) and sketch (opposite page)

This exchange and sharing can be seen very clearly in the **Pessac project**. Known also as *Quartier Frugès* or *Quartier des Monteil*, located near Bordeaux, it involved sixty units of low-middle-class housing. Henry Frugès commissioned the project in 1924. A millionaire involved in the timber and sugar industries, Frugès was not an ordinary entrepreneur. He composed music, painted, designed fabrics, and was also an art collector. He saw Pessac as an experimental development of a garden city providing for the market a kind of house "in the pure air of the pine forest" that was not yet considered possible. Le Corbusier found in it the opportunity of a laboratory. Most of Le Corbusier's experiments involved the technology of construction. Architecturally, he mostly applied prototypes he had previously conceived in fabric. Le Corbusier thought that the site of Pessac was too drab to leave the concrete houses without color. Drawing from his experience as a painter, he developed a palette of tones that he considered fit for the landscape. Five years later, he would repeat the experiment with Villa Savoye.

Construction began in 1925 and ended in 1926. Frugès did not expect Le Corbusier to produce a conventional plan or to follow traditional construction methods. His ambition was to reform the conservative practices of French architects and contractors who provided commercial housing. Both Le Corbusier and M. Frugès failed to realize how unrealistic their expectations were. There were problems with the local administration services. They ignored products and skills available locally, opting for novel experimental methods for prefabrication. A Parisian enterprise replaced the inadequate local contractors and workers who could not cope with the difficulties of the new construction technology

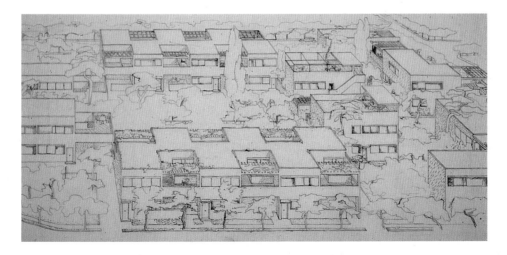

that Le Corbusier and Frugés wanted to apply and that involved cement gun equipment and untested techniques. Other major mistakes were made: the water supply was inadequate, the cost was high, the price was wrong, the amount of space supplied too small. And for months, the houses remained unoccupied. In his Œuvre, Le Corbusier later characterized their efforts as reminiscient of Balzac's tragic herœs. Although avant-garde architects such as Walter Gropius, who visited the project in 1926, were fascinated, Pessac was a technological, functional, and financial failure. Frugès himself had a breakdown and retired from work in 1929.

V

Le Corbusier wrote in his Œuvre Complète how, in 1922, five years after he had settled in Paris, the director of the "urban section" of the Salon D'Automne invited him to design "something" for the exhibition. Asked by Le Corbusier to clarify what he meant by urbanism, the director cited examples of what we call today "urban furniture," such as a fountain in a square. Le Corbusier accepted the offer by saying that he was willing to design a fountain with a "city for three million people" behind it as a background. Thus, following his professional principle not to let go the opportunity the humblest commission would offer, he proceeded to present his ideas on urbanism on a big scale. More than an expression of imperialism, Le Corbusier's proposal had the goal to redefine the idea of the city and to reintroduce the new field of urbanism. The show consisted of a 27-meter-long stand displaying theoretical diagrams and a plan for a **Contemporary City of Three Million People** ("Ville Contemporaine"), presented through drawings and a 100-square-meters diorama. The project was exhibited without much verbal

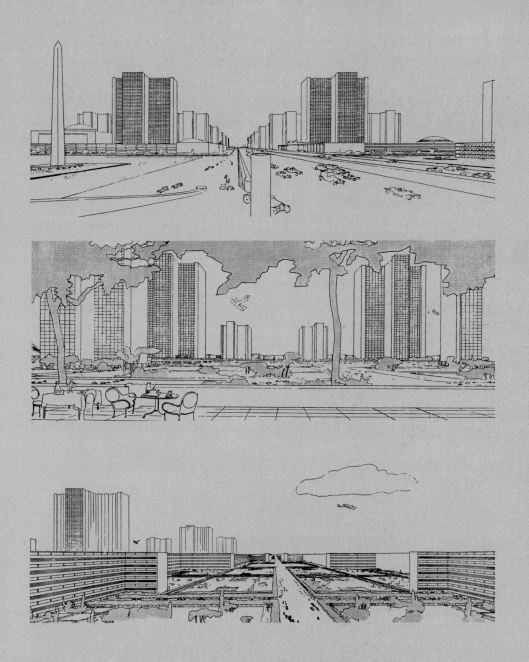

Cité-Jardin Frugès: view of housing blocks (opposite page), photograph by Lucien Herve; Ville Contemporaine, 1922 (above)

explanation. That was provided in Le Corbusier's 1925 book *Urbanisme,* which offered a justification of the plans, backing figures, and explicit goals behind the project.

Le Corbusier's plan provided for a city center to be occupied by 400,000 inhabitants within twenty-four 60-story-high skyscrapers. A 250-meter open area surrounded every skyscraper, and a continuous green park zone, equipped with recreational facilities for communal use, was reserved for future development around this center. The plan also provided for six double-story apartments to accommodate 600,000 inhabitants. They were arranged in a series of meandering slabs (*redents*) that were elevated on *pilotis.* Finally, there was a development of garden cities for two million inhabitants around the circumference of the scheme.

The same analytical approach Le Corbusier adopted in the design of villas or housing guided him in developing projects for a newly born area of investigation, *urbanism.* Traditional categories were eliminated. The street was purged. So were the traditional types of buildings that accompanied it. The city was divided in its constituent elements, rearranged rationally according to new targets: decongesting the center, increasing the density, increasing the means of circulation, and increasing the planted surface. As stated by Le Corbusier, "a city made for speed is a city made for success." The center of the plan was occupied by a metro station with three underground levels intended as a station for suburban trains and for trains for distant destinations. A mezzanine level was set aside for the automobiles and a 200,000-square-meter platform served as an airport.

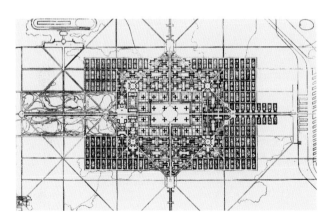

Ville Contemporaine: view of model
(above), courtesy Fondation Le
Corbusier; plan (opposite page)

The new prototypes used in the Ville Contemporaine were: a very tall cross-shaped skyscraper, the *redents,* and the **Immeubles Villa** block. We can see Le Corbusier's combined reuse of precedents in the conception of the Immeubles Villa. The "new formula" for high-rise living in the Immeubles Villa came about by stacking up the two-story "boxes" of the Citrohan house for twelve floors and then attaching the solarium, providing an elevated garden terrace for each duplex. The inhabitants of the Immeubles have no servants, and everyday shopping is no longer done along the streets. Redrawing the Chartreuse d'Ema precedent, Le Corbusier instead made all such services communal. Working day and night, they were centralized in each apartment block organizationally, functionally, and spatially.

The Immeubles Villa living unit was finally worked out in detail and realized as a prototype in the form of the **Pavillon de L'Esprit Nouveau,** which was commissioned and built for the Exposition des Arts Décoratifs held in Paris in 1925. Constructed by standardized industrial elements, it was divided into two side-by-side parts, a prototype apartment and an exhibition about the idea itself. The residential unit was furnished by Thone pieces, among others, and included paintings by Léger, Gris, and Ozenfant on its walls. Part of it was an enclosed garden with an emblematic tree growing in the middle, which, in the real project, was expected to be nurtured into maturity. The pavillion was not received without controversy. Its purist character appeared even more iconoclastic given the context of the exhibition and its objective to show examples of traditional decorative arts. Writing about the show, the Russian writer Ilya Ehrenburg called the French pavilions gray and drab, the Italian arrogant

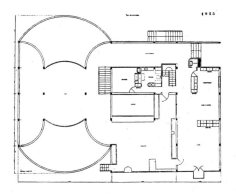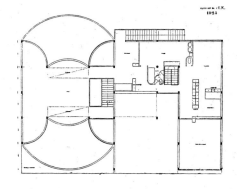

Immeubles Villa project, 1925 (opposite page): detail of courtyards in the air (bottom)
Pavillon de L'Espirit Nouveau, Paris, 1925: ground and first floor plans (above)

L'ESPRIT
NOUVEAU

and stupid, and the Soviet, by Konstantin Melnikov, "not an assertion of utilitarianism, with an impossible stair and no protection from rain." Ehrenburg noted that the Le Corbusier pavillion was the only one that stood out. The structure was demolished immediately after the show was over. In 1977 it was reconstructed by the city of Bologna.

Initially, Le Corbusier proposed to the industrialist and innovator André-Gustave Citroën that he sponsor a revolutionary, colossal project: a redevelopment of Paris to be exhibited in the Pavillon de L'Esprit Nouveau at the Exposition des Arts Décoratifs. The "automobile destroyed the city, the automobile will save it," Le Corbusier argued. It was the second time he had tried to attract the attention of Citroën after exploiting his near name for the Maison Citrohan in 1922. But Citroën was not moved. Thus, the 1925 study bore the name of another constructor of airplanes and automobiles. It came to be known as the **Plan Voisin**.

Two years before, in a text accompanying the massive project for the reconstruction of Paris, exhibited in the Pavillon de L'Esprit Nouveau, Le Corbusier paid homage to Louis XIV, whom Le Corbusier called the "first urbanist of the West." At the same time, he pleaded for the introduction of a "modern sensitivity," a "new attitude" favoring the "geometric spirit, a spirit of construction and synthesis." That meant "exactitude and order," the "banal," the "common," and "the limpid fact" rather than the individualistic, "the product of fever." For him, that spirit was to be found in the work of Bach, not Wagner, and in the Pantheon, not the cathedral.

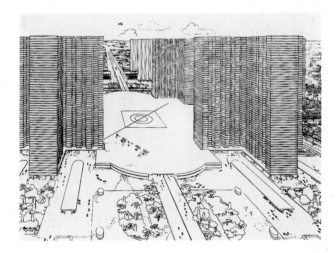

Pavillon de L'Espirit Nouveau (opposite page); Plan Voisin for Paris, 1925 (right)

In design terms, the idea of the geometric spirit was expressed in a rigorous rectilinear grid coordinate system, a strict separation between built volumes and green open areas, and wide highways meeting at right angles. In this new world the street had "ceased to exist." Those "gloomy clefts," those "appalling nightmares," Le Corbusier wrote, have been replaced by "widely spaced" cross-shaped "crystal towers," "translucent prisms" that "soar higher than any pinnacle on earth." There was no brick and stone seen only in "glass and … proportion." Lower slab buildings, running along a zig-zag pattern, accompanied the tall towers. Green was everywhere, not only between the towers but also in the skyscrapers and in roof gardens, 200 meters above ground, "planted with spindleberries, thuyas, laurels, and ivy" and even "beds of tulips." Not all was destroyed of old Paris. In the midst of the planted areas, Le Corbusier left the old churches or mansions of the Marais freestanding and still active. Ramps and raised pedestrian walkways, flanked by long stretches of shops and cafés, overlooking the grounds, linked the buildings. Automobiles serviced the city and ample parking was provided for them. In addition there was an underground metro and an airport on the top of it, raised like the towers on *pilotis*. Le Corbusier imagined the city to have "clear and pure air," to be free of noise, and to provide its inhabitants with the spectacle of cars "crossing Paris at lightning speed," leaving during the night "luminous tracks … like the tails of meteors."

As the 1920s came to an end, Le Corbusier's fame spread around the world. In 1927 he built a version of the Maison Citrohan prototypes in the city of Stuttgart for the Colony of Weissenhof Development. He was invited to lecture in Madrid and Barcelona. In 1928, he lectured in Moscow,

Plan Voisin: aerial view of model,
courtesy Fondation Le Corbusier

and in June, with others, he founded the Congrès Internationaux d'Architecture Moderne (International Congresses of Modern Architecture; CIAM) at La Sarraz Castle in Switzerland. In 1929, he returned to lecture tours, this time in South America, and he visited Moscow again and made his first professional journey to Algiers.

Together with these successes, the decade, close to its end, brought a major disappointment, the loss of the commission for the League of Nations headquarters in Geneva, a competition Le Corbusier had won. In his career, it stood as the beginning of a new phase related to large-scale institutional buildings of a public character. The rejection was a major professional setback and Le Corbusier did not miss the opportunity to chronicle it, heroize it, and make the best publicity of his mission out of it. He published the account of his failure in *Une maison – un palais* ("A House – A Palace"), in which he presented his ideas for a modern "palace." He also included it as the first volume of his *Œuvre Complète,* edited by Willy Boesiger and published in 1929. The editor's role was extremely important yet it is worth noting that, up to very recently, the best books one could read about Le Corbusier were written, directly or indirectly, by Le Corbusier himself. In 1930 Le Corbusier became a French citizen and married Yvonne Gallis.

Plan Voisin: aerial view of model,
courtesy Fondation Le Corbusier

"Palaces," "Seascrapers," "Virgilian Dreams"   **CHAPTER** 03

I

The chronicle of Le Corbusier's work, as he recorded in his *Œuvre*, identifies the decade between 1920 and 1930 as the first period of his practice. However, in his introduction to the second volume of the *Œuvre*, Le Corbusier suggests a different division, the decade division starting with his arrival in Paris in 1908 and terminating in 1927. As he wrote about his practice in Paris, "till 1927 we were only two, Pierre Jeanneret and myself. From that time on, our circle steadily grew." His practice did not increase only in terms of people; the scale of projects that the office undertook expanded too. With the exception of Pessac, during his first ten years in Paris, Le Corbusier built only small buildings. His large projects, like the Immeubles Villas or Plan Voisin, were theoretical. On the other hand, designing these modest buildings during 1917 and 1927 was not independent of conceiving of the bigger and more complex projects he produced during the next decade. The decade between 1917 and 1927 was a period of "patient research" – to use Le Corbusier's expression. Using data collected during the previous decade (1907–1917), when he was a traveler and an apprentice, Le Corbusier dedicated his research to the critique of traditional architectural language and to the development of new concepts, such as the piloti, the roof garden, and the free plan. The villas served as laboratory cases for exploration and testing of methodological tools for a broader practice to come.

The first time Le Corbusier came very close to building a large, complex project was when he won the competition for the **Palace of the League of Nations** for Geneva in 1927. Unfortunately, "intrigues,"

Palace of the League of Nations,
Geneva, Switzerland, 1927

in the words of Le Corbusier, "deprived (him and Pierre Jeanneret) of the fruit of their labors." With the formal excuse that he had used "printers-ink instead of chinese ink," to draw the plans, "the building was awarded to four academic architects."

Having lost on a technicality, Le Corbusier protested. He tried legal means as well as publicity, but to no avail. If he lost the commission in the world of glass, concrete, and steel, he definitely won it in the perhaps more enduring world of words and historical memory. He wrote about the affair in his first volume of his *Œuvre* in 1929. In the year before, he had devoted a whole book to the subject: *Une maison – un palais*. What made these "auto-historical" documents have an enduring fascination was that beyond polemics they dealt with problems of design theory and methodology, revealing Le Corbusier's architectural thinking and design creative process. *Une maison – un palais,* subtitled *À la recherche d'une unité architectural* ("In search of an architectural unity"), presents explicitly the relationship between the Villa-laboratory investigations and the new large-scale problems, using the Palace of the League of Nations as an example. The book shows how the *pilotis* and the roof garden were applied during 1927 to the Weissenhof Development and to the palace. The same point was made about the new concept of surface openings, *fenêtre en longuer*, applied in the Villa Garches and the "organic" plan schema applied in the Villa La Roche; both were implemented in the Geneva Palace.

S. D. N.

Interestingly, in 1930, in *Précisions*, the "organic" La Roche plan scheme, characterized by putting all spatial-functional divisions – the "organs" – next to one another without any external configurational constraints – to use Le Corbusier's words, "the inside taking its ease pushing out to form a variation of projections" – can fail. If "one does not watch out," it can become "picturesque" and "easy," both of which Le Corbusier viewed as negative qualities. Le Corbusier juxtaposed the plan of Villa La Roche to that of Villa Savoye – which he thought was superior – so that all building organs were compressed in a rigid external envelop but also adequately free to obey their internal functional configurational requirements. However, the La Roche prototype was much easier to use for a building of the size and functional complexity of the palace. It permitted greater freedom to cope with operational requirements. As in Villa Meyer, Le Corbusier took the circulation "organ" out of the volume of the palace and gave it a shape that would conform to the function. He did the same with the 2,600-person auditorium – he removed it from the rest of the complex, giving it a contour derived from acoustics, as interpreted by a specialist, Gustave Lyon. The 500 offices, their long windows using Saint-Gobain glass, were also arranged to accommodate the need for direct access from the outside and for abundance of light. Le Corbusier placed them on *pilotis* and turned the space under into a parking lot, an unprecedented decision that was shocking at that time. The dangers of "picturesqueness" and "easiness" inherent in this prototype were avoided, as they were in Villa La Roche, by rendering space divisions according to the discipline of the classical canon. Again, as in the Villa La Roche, the canon was applied in a subtle way, taking liberties whenever functions had to be accommodated and violating it at local but critical points to avoid worn, routine compositional effects. While many

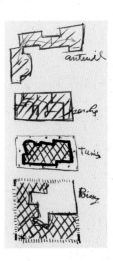

Palace of the League of Nations (opposite page): aerial view (top) and perspective sketch (bottom); Four plan types, *Précisions*, Paris, 1930 (right)

classical precedents probably assisted in Le Corbusier's conception of the Geneva Palace scheme, one seems to have played the most important role: the Palace of Versailles.

Professionally, Le Corbusier made the best use of the rejection of his Geneva Palace entry, turning it into a moving force behind many of his career and ideological campaigns. Using it as a complete example of a new way of thinking about buildings, he established an agenda of six urgent questions on modern technique and its consequences, standardization, economy, urbanism, education of the youth, and the state of architecture, and in 1928 he mobilized a number of young architects already involved in the modernist movement as a pressure group and as a group for reflection.

Despite the fact that the Le Corbusier project for the Geneva Palace had deep roots in classicism, the architect who won the prize announced publicly that he considered his personal victory as "a beautiful victory against barbarity!" That gave Le Corbusier every opportunity to aim his vitriol against the establishment at large. Within this context, it is no surprise that in October 1928, a year after the Geneva fiasco, he was lecturing in the most antiestablishment center, Moscow, U.S.S.R., having won the competition for **Centrosoyuz**, the central office of the Union of the Coopératives in U.R.S.S., a quintessential Bolshevik institution. The Centrosoyuz, a facility for 2,500 employees, became the first major project by Le Corbusier to be built. A small group of dedicated admirers in Russia that contributed to his victory, including the brothers Leonid and Alexander Vesnin and Moisej Ginsburg, expected to offer to the Soviet public a demonstration of what modern architecture could achieve,

Centrosoyuz, Moscow, U.S.S.R, 1927,
photo courtesy of Michael Levin

through Le Corbusier, an outsider whose reputation was already established internationally. Le Corbusier, in turn, although the journal *L'Humanité* viciously criticized his work, maintained friendly ties with other communists, French and Russian. Ilya Ehrenburg, as we have seen, admired his work, and *L'Esprit Nouveau* published his articles as well as projects by Soviet constructivists, such as Vladimir Tatlin's Monument for the Third International. As Le Corbusier stated in August 10, 1934, in a letter to A. Vesnin, he then believed that the U.S.S.R. could "provide magnificent and unique opportunities ... (and that) it is important that contemporary architecture not only finds its place there, but also its true expression."

The Centrosoyuz plan evolved through stages. First, Le Corbusier divided the program into simple, elementary, functional parts and then struggled to arrange them to fit to the site configuration and to meet the requirements of the internal organization. In comparison to the Palace of the League of Nations, Le Corbusier was less interested in arranging the parts of Centrosoyuz as a formal composition. Given the scale of the crowds that would use the building and the special organizational constraints needed to channel the visitors to their destinations, his major concern was circulation. An elaborate system of ramps was developed, the *architectural promenade* assuming a special political significance. As with the Geneva Palace, the auditorium, shaped according to scientifically established acoustic determinants, was articulated as a "differentiated organ," and stuck out from the mass of architectural elements.

During his second trip to Moscow in 1929, Le Corbusier came as close as one could be to the Soviet power. He met Stalin in the Kremlin, although it appears the encounter did not inspire Le Corbusier

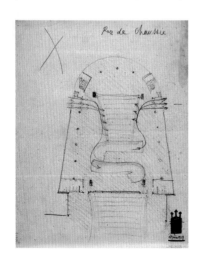

Centrosoyuz: model (above) and
sketch (opposite page), both courtesy
Fondation Le Corbusier

much or help him to have his way as a professional: Centrosoyuz was not built exactly the way Le Corbusier wanted it. One of Le Corbusier's ambitions for this project was to construct a building as a completely sealed, scientifically controlled environment. "The authorities," however, as Le Corbusier referred to his Soviet clients, did not approve the idea. A few years later, a capitalist institution would give him the opportunity to apply his innovative idea, that of "exact respiration" for buildings "hermetically sealed." In the interim, however, Le Corbusier was offered a commission of another large building in 1930: the **Pavillon Suisse**.

As if to counterbalance the Soviet commission, as well as the injustice carried out against Le Corbusier by the League of Nations in a Swiss city, the committee of Swiss universities appointed Le Corbusier to design the Pavillon Suisse. The program asked for a building containing housing and social services for Swiss university students in Paris. Located in the Cité Universitaire in the fourteenth section of Paris – not a particularly attractive location at that time – the site had soil problems, and an extremely tight budget. Le Corbusier once more faced a difficult but irresistible challenge.

The plan Le Corbusier conceived for this building was once more "organic." The building was divided into independent articulated parts, or "organs": the slab housing the students sat on robust concrete *pilotis* and the entry and communal spaces, plus the concierge quarters, appear to be part of the circulation tower containing the stair and the elevator. More than in any earlier project, Le Corbusier used a number of different materials, such as glass, stone, and concrete, in varied textures. The structure of the slab on

Pavillon Suisse, Cité Universitaire, Paris,
1930–1932, courtesy Lucien Herve

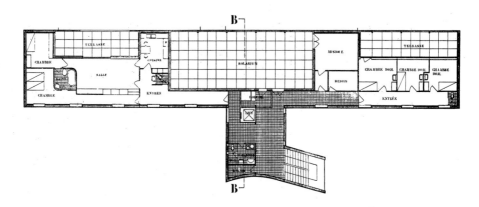

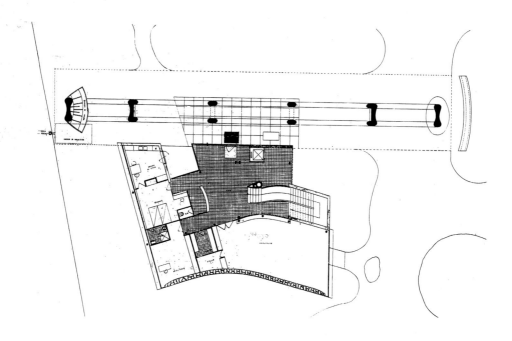

Pavillon Suisse: ground floor plan (bottom) and first floor plan (top)

Pavillon Suisse: view through the *pilotis*,
courtesy Fondation Le Corbusier

pilotis followed the Dom-ino principle, a frame independent of the facade and dividing interior walls. Each dormitory unit was constructed as an independent floating entity, following the analogy of a "bottle in a bottlerack," a generic analogy he will apply again in the end of the 1940s for the Unité d'Habitation.

The building performed relatively well and there were no major crises. However, Le Corbusier once more was the subject of controversy. Following his compulsion to recall the act of parental rejection and the temptation to use the rejection as an opportunity to attack authority, he exposed its stupidity and intolerance, and subsequently indulged in self-aggrandizement. In his *Œuvre,* Le Corbusier dedicated a whole page to publicizing the attacks against the project. He reproduced in its entirety an article from *Gazette de Lausanne* that was published six months after the inauguration of the building, on December 28, 1933. The text assailed him for "abduction of minors" and called the building a piece of "propaganda," perilous to the intellectual and moral development of the young Swiss. It accused Le Corbusier of being dishonest and misleading. By Le Corbusier claiming that it was "spiritual," the project actually promoted materialism through its forms and displays. As key evidence of that, the article targeted the photomurals used by Le Corbusier depicting nature, mostly close-ups of inorganic or organic forms, as well as material from "Russian USSR, illustrated magazines."

Just a year before this accusation, in 1932, Le Corbusier had been commissioned for the third time by a philanthropic, rather conservative institution, the Salvation Army in Paris, to design **La Cité de Refuge**, a shelter for the homeless. It was the third and most important commission Le Corbusier

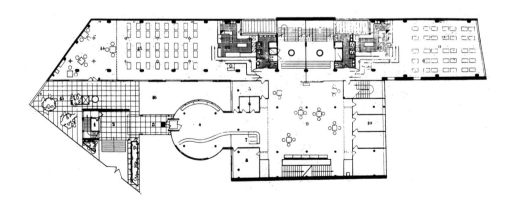

La Cité de Refuge, Paris, 1932 (above),
courtesy Fondation Le Corbusier; entrance
plan (opposite page)

received from the Salvation Army. An important ally in this project, as in the previous two, was Princess Winaretta de Polignac-Singer, for whom Le Corbusier had designed a villa in 1926 that was never built. Despite this, she remained his supporter.

Again, Le Corbusier was faced with a difficult site, an unprecedented program, and a very tight budget. The scheme was broken down into the public realm, further analyzed in elementary functions that were assigned into individual volumes, and the private realm, the individual living cells for the homeless. Once more the Dom-ino prototype was applied. The last two levels of the volume were broken into smaller units, with a shift in the angle of the facade, creating an effect that may have been admirable by contemporary standards but was imposed for zoning reasons – it was not by Le Corbusier's own choice.

The important innovations of the project were mainly technical. Le Corbusier used widely the so-called Nevada glass brick that was introduced by the famous French glass manufacturer Saint-Gobain in 1928. Pierre Chareau had already used it in the construction of the Maison de Verre ("Glass House"), in the very beginning of the 1930s. It is known that Le Corbusier passed by that site everyday on his way to work while it was under construction and witnessed the way the all-glass walls were built, step by step. Glass bricks became one of his most beloved materials for the rest of his life. Another significant innovation was the 16.5-meters-high by 57-meters-long glass curtain wall on the south facade of La Cité de Refuge. Le Corbusier's most important technological innovation was the conception of the

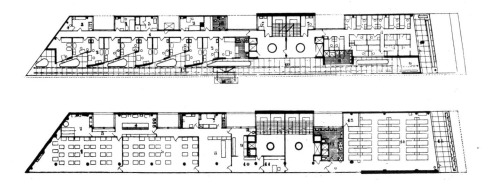

La Cité de Refuge: corner detail (opposite page), photograph by Michael Levin;
top floor plan with apartments for mothers with children (top); dormitory floor plan (bottom)

building as a completely controlled environmental system. Le Corbusier's application of the idea was already used for cinemas and public buildings, mostly in the United States, but it was rarely employed for housing.

Construction on La Cité started in June 1930. The concrete structure finished on time; the rest of the construction was delayed, resulting from the novelty of the technology and Le Corbusier's lack of precision in his shop drawings. Finally, in December 1933, the President of the Republic inaugurated the building. It was the coldest day of the last thirty years, a hard test for the experimental all-glass facade. Le Corbusier wrote that the building passed the test, but the real story was different. There were numerous serious post-occupancy complaints and many changes were necessary to make the climatic controls work.

While still working on the Pavillon Suisse, Le Corbusier was asked by the Soviet government to submit a design for the **Palace of the Soviets** in Moscow, on the occasion of the Five-Year Plan, in 1931. More than any other project by Le Corbusier, the palace came close to resembling a assemblage of anatomical organs or a machine. The configuration emerged out of the analysis of the program into specialized, differentiated functional units. Each type of elementary unit was given its articulated form, according to its functional constraints. All units were put together within an "organic" type of scheme, that is, they were combined to fit external site constraints and internal interconnection needs. Le Corbusier worked hard to generate and evaluate a series of alternative combinatorial arrangements.

Palace of the Soviets (above); apartment building, rue Nungesser-et-Coli, Paris, 1933 (opposite page), photograph by Michael Levin

The scheme chosen in the end was the clearest organizationally. But it was also the closest to the classical canon, with rigorous tripartite divisions ordering the spatial disposition of the functional units making the complex more imagineable and memorable.

The palace was to operate as a congress center of high political significance. The program included an auditorium for 15,000 people with a gigantic scene for 1,500 actors. There were halls and restaurants to support the events. Le Corbusier stated that he paid special attention to a gigantic vestiary, to accommodate the heavy overcoats and hats worn by men and women during the Russian winter. A second auditorium, for 6,500 people, was also part of the project and was dedicated to meetings of the Third International, during which conferences were taking place alternating with theater, music, and other cultural events, for which there were two more halls for 500 people and two for 200. Following his already established principles, Le Corbusier analyzed the complex into elements of: (1) Structure, the skeleton, (2) Organs, the assembly spaces, and (3) Circulation, inclined passages, ramps, corridors, and stairs.

Concerning structure, each functional unit was given its own spanning system. Le Corbusier suspended their roofs on the two halls making them visually the preeminent parts of the complex. In a brilliant move, as a Brunelleschi of our times, Le Corbusier hung half of the roof of the major hall from an arch, thus inventing a modern alternative to the traditional dome. Certainly, the 50-meter-high and 300-meter-span arches of the Orly hangar used by Eugène Freyssinet in 1921 must have been a

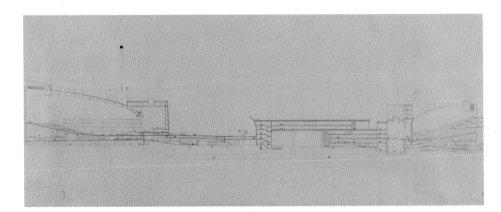

precedent for Le Corbusier's scheme. However, the most significant part of the conception followed the approach already used in the Dom-ino. As the traditional wall was divided into two specialized elements there – the skeleton and the "free" facade – so was the historical dome, the skeleton of the arch and the "free" roof covering suspended from it. The analogy between the two was made explicit in the drawing published in his *Œuvre*, in which Le Corbusier presented a sketch of the project next to a sketch of the historical center of Pisa.

The intricacy of the circulation in the Palace of the Soviets resulted from the complexity of the ceremonial, bureaucratic, and security requirements of the political meetings and the different groups participating in the meetings. Le Corbusier's ambition was to invent a true machine to carry out mass politics. He aspired to a building whose form, resulting from "mathematical calculations" – which guided the form of the great hall and its arch in his scheme – would lead to an "impeccable harmony, a magnificence similar to that of the forms of nature" emblematic in its truth of the New Times. His ambition was not fulfilled. "Abruptly," the commission was given to the designer, who came up with a solution that was designed according styles of the Italian Renaissance. Le Corbusier's scheme was accused of resembling a factory. Surprisingly, not only did Le Corbusier not complain, he appeared to understand the situation then characterizing the U.S.S.R. – it was an underdeveloped nation in need of more reassuring public settings than historicist architecture could supply. His attitude when it came to similar problems in other underdeveloped parts of the world, such as South America or Algiers, would be very different.

Palace of the Soviets (above and opposite)

II

The same kind of reframing from Le Corbusier's architectural thinking of buildings that took place during the decade between 1917 and 1927 occurred in reference to the urban environment. There was a critique of traditional architectural language leading to the rejection of the concept of "street," "center," and "building," as distinct from "city." There was a development of new elements of design analysis, division of parts, and their recombination into new concepts, tools for design. In contrast to the production of a large number of villas during this decade that served as laboratory cases for later large-scale applications, there is nothing equivalent for the urban scale. In this respect, the "patient research," as we find it in the Plan Voisin, remained theoretical.

During the decade between 1927 and 1937, during which he was involved with large buildings, Le Corbusier sought for opportunities to apply his newly developed theories about the city and the region. As France seemed unresponsive to these ideas, he became engaged in an almost frantic program of global traveling and lecturing. In addition to Russia, where Le Corbusier was busy with individual buildings, the main focus of his visits included Argentina, Brazil, the United States, and Algiers, countries that he thought offered significant opportunities for getting commissions and finding followers. No such commissions ever arrived. However, in addition to spreading his ideas, there was a major gain for Le Corbusier. Being always an explorer, a student, and a collector of new objects for his thesaurus, he looked at these voyages as opportunities for constant learning. In Russia, he received ideas from avant-garde architects and artists. In America and Africa, he acquired precedents from local architecture.

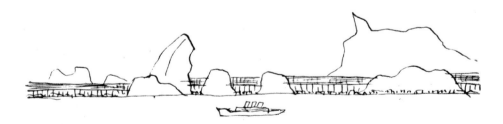

In 1929, while still working on U.S.S.R. projects and on Villa Savoye, Le Corbusier accepted invitations to visit and to lecture in South America. From the very beginning, the voyage appeared to be an inspiring experience. He spent most of his fourteen days crossing the ocean via what he declared several times to be his favored environment, a liner, the *Giulio Cesare.* Liners fascinated him because they were a technological feat and because they combined two extremes: very stern private cells with lush public spaces and a joy of life with a sense of community. Aboard the ship, he met Josephine Baker. Already a world famous performer, Baker was also renowned for her depth and brilliance. A dear of many Parisian intellectuals, she evidently had a major impact on Le Corbusier's mood and thinking. Le Corbusier drew her in several stages of undress but also discussed with her problems of culture, as is revealed from his susbequent writings in *Précisions – a* book written during his later days in South America. Writings and drawings produced during this voyage surpass in sensuality anything he did before. But what is even more dominant in them is his protest, occasionally vitriolic, against racism and his admiration of the cultures of blacks and the dispossessed. Far from romantic, "orientalist," or politically militant, they emerge out of the *cathare* sense of roseate dissidence and a certain noblesse oblige.

South America gave him the feeling of immensity – "an immense light" and an "immense land" such as he had never experienced. Invited by the South American Aviation Company, he flew over almost the entire continent: Argentina, Paraguay, Uruguay, Brazil, the pampas, the "great floods of the Parana," the "wrinkled skin of the Cordillera of the Andes," the tropical forest. During his flights, he asked the

Views of Seascrapers, Rio, 1929

pilots for special routes so as to examine specific aspects of the landscape. One of his pilots was the famous author of *Le Petit Prince*, Antoine de Saint-Exupéry. "From the plane, one understands," stated Le Corbusier. Flying at 1,200 meters, new worlds emerge. It is possible for "eyes to see" the world of "biology," of "organic life," and of the physical law "of the steepest gradient" determining the flow of water and the "theorem of the meander." But it is also possible to perceive the levels of the city, to see "where it rises, and where it stacks up its floors as the result of the irresistible push of business." "When one has taken a long flight ... like a bird gliding," Le Corbusier reflected, "ideas attack you." They enabled him to reconcile prototypes he had already developed with precedents from the thesaurus of his travels to conceive new prototypes. The "apartment villas," the zig-zag slabs (*redent*-block) of the Plan Voisin, the Dom-ino house, as well as the regalia of *pilotis*, gardens up in the air, free plan and free facade, together with the Roman viaduct and the ocean liner were recombined into "majestic" "seascrapers" and "earthscrapers," colossal multilevel, multifunctional linear structures. The gridiron schema of the Plan Voisin was melted down to adapt to the topography of the area. "From the plane," he envisioned the "megastructures" spanning "from hill to hill, from summit to summit" – "bigger than the aqueduct of Segovia" and holding expressways on the top, incorporating offices in the middle, and leaving the ground "free for sports and parking" – raising housing that "would start only at 30 meters above the ground ... up to 100 meters above the ground of the city or more." Le Corbusier thought that by raising the built volume 30 meters, the structure would "avoid disturbing anyone." Further on, Le Corbusier believed that this height would guarantee the best quality air, free from pollution and humidity. During his lecture tour, hoping to open the cities to the sea and sky, he proposed versions

of this prototype for Buenos Aires, São Paulo, and Rio de Janeiro. He would expand and apply these ideas two years later in *Précisions*.

He lectured on these ideas, improvising, sketching on big pieces of paper with big strokes, and making the public "feel that (he) created for it." Between lectures and meetings, he walked around and visited places as he had during his previous trips in Europe. During these walks, he recorded the value of the regional structures, the "cardboard richness and Latin smile" of the "balusters" appearing everywhere. He also reflected on the threat of the global, the "enormous pressure USA exercises, by its ships, its capital, and its engineers" and the resulting "houses in corrugated sheet metal, without a heart or a soul." He contrasted the sterile international style of the luxury restaurants and their "inevitable order" with the deeper wisdom of "houses of plain people," and he was overcome by thoughts that remind him of Rousseau – that "man is good." But when he thought "of architects" his thoughts were more like Voltaire's – that "all is for the worst in the most hateful of worlds."

It was spring when Le Corbusier arrived in Argentina and tropical summer when he arrived in Brazil. He studied the natural landscape and collected precedents of local structures improvised by poor people, mostly black. His ideas were not of a romantic "exoticist." He wrote with respect and admiration about the blacks. Climbing the hills inhabited by them "to find their house ... almost always on the edge of the cliff," he remarked, "there is pride in the eye of the black ... the eye of the man who sees wise horizons ... the thought of the planner." Le Corbusier reported that "important Brazilian personages"

Sketches for the Expansion of Rio de Janiero, Brazil, 1929–1932

Le Corbusier with Lucio Cost and
Oscar Niemeyer: Ministry of Public
Education, Rio de Janiero, Brazil,
1936, photograph by Lucien Herve

were shocked to learn about his escapades, informing him how dangerous these neighborhoods were. Le Corbusier's response was that he was not afraid of them, because "they only kill the thief of love, he who wounded them profoundly." These warnings reminded him of similar warnings he heard before about the "Turks," that "they will kill" him. Yet, nothing happened to him; the memory of Stamboul remained as a place "warming … the … heart" juxtaposed to the Acropolis of Athens, which stood for monumentality, harmony with the landscape, and abstract mathematical thinking.

No commission on the urban scale resulted out of these lectures. In 1936, however, Le Corbusier was invited to Brazil once more. On his way there, he flew the *Count Zeppelin,* where he wasted no time to explore its design and to find that everything the German engineers designed abided by his rules. In Brazil, he was asked to design the **Ministry of Public Education** in collaboration with Lucio Costa and Oscar Niemeyer. The scheme reused the arrangements of the majestic halls proposed for the Palace of the Soviets in Moscow, giving them an even greater sense of splendor. The most important innovation of the scheme was the use of "sunbreaks" that would be further developed in his work in Algiers half a decade later.

III

Le Corbusier's involvement with the urban plan of the city of Algiers followed immediately after his urbanization studies in 1930 in South America. He continued to visit the city almost every year until the middle of World War II without ever receiving a commission or even having a major impact on local architecture and planning. Algiers, like South America and the U.S.S.R., appealed to Le Corbusier. It appeared to be a place full of both potential and problems, thus promising for the application of new architectural ideas. In addition, August Perret, whose innovative work in concrete Le Corbusier admired, had already been there and managed to receive commissions. And, as in the U.S.S.R. and in South America, there was a small but dynamic group of architects who knew his ideas from his publications and who were interested in promoting these ideas. One of these architects, Pierre-André Emery, received Le Corbusier when he first arrived and guided him around the magnificent sites of the city, including the Casbah, a visit that impressed Le Corbusier tremendously.

The city of Algiers, a vital port opening as a vast white amphitheater to the Mediterranean, was expanding rapidly at that moment. Its population consisted of 250,000 people. Two-thirds of the population were Europeans living in relatively modern quarters that were serviced by broad boulevards. The rest were Muslim and resided in the Casbah, an unclean maze of constricted alleys and densely crammed dwellings. Le Corbusier's objective was to develop a scheme to "permit this city, actually in a dramatic impasse, to find the necessary means to expand." The first proposal, known as "plan A," was a "grenade project," as Le Corbusier and Pierre Jeanneret called it, and was aimed to shake up the planning authorities and make them aware of radical alternatives. It consisted of three components: a new "business city," at the extremity of the Algiers cape; a "residential city" on Fort-l'Empereur, an inaccessible area at that moment; and a link between the two suburbs located at the extremities of Algiers at St-Eugène and Hussein-Dey. The link component was an "earthscraper," similar in conception

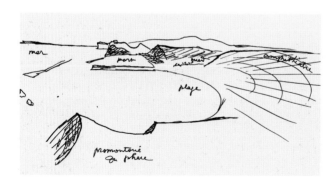

to the ones he proposed for the South American cities. The highway was raised 60 to 90 meters above the ground. Inside its supporting concrete structure he proposed to insert housing for 180,000 people. However, Le Corbusier produced a number of drawings in which he explored the potential of the system manifesting the extremes of freedom of choice from the Dom-ino schema of supports and platforms enabling people to choose the kind of house they wanted. Two drawings have been saved in the Fondation Le Corbusier archive where one can see almost cartoonlike exaggerations of the variety of individual units accomodated inside the structure. Since the end of World War II, many architects were inspired by the drawings, including John Habraken and Kenzo Tange, and through them the influence is still felt today.

The 1934 proposal for the **Urbanization of Nemours,** a town in Algiers that was initially laid out by the French colonial army in 1850, was studied in cooperation with H. Breuillot and Pierre-André Emery, who was responsible for the commission. Le Corbusier proposed a new town of 50,000 inhabitants that he considered prototypical, complying with the resolutions of the Fourth International Congress for Modern Architecture, held in Athens in July 1933. He noted, however, that he saw in the scheme a contemporary interpretation of regionalist architecture – an architecture, as he stated in La Chaux-de-Fonds in his last disputes with Charles L'Eplattenier, that in a machine-age civilization can no longer be "born" spontaneously. It must be carried out through a "plan." *Regionalist* architecture, like the one "of Île-de-France, ... Brittany, ... Provence ... the Casbah in Algiers, ... the Swiss Chalet," Le Corbusier commented, "shares the integrity of nature, exalts each site, opens the soul of the site, is embodied

Project from A, B, C and H, the Urbanization of Nemours, Algiers

in the site." It is based on *topography* and *orientation.* These qualities, disappearing now, because only "money makes the laws," Le Corbusier claimed, can be recaptured through the *plan*. The plan Le Corbusier proposed was a hierarchical system of segregated layers of circulation. It consisted of the through traffic, a 12-meter structure above the ground. Embodied in it is the *souk,* the market and depots. Under it is the local traffic, interwoven with pedestrian circulation. Finally, there is the long-haul water and rail traffic. An essential part of the system is that it is layered in time; it is constructed in stages. The inhabitants were to be housed in eighteen high-rise slab-shaped buildings that were turned toward the best orientation laid out in an amphitheatrical form that overlooked the Mediterranean. The rigorous division of functions and specialization of areas and urban organs based on the latest technology was applied further to segregate the areas of habitation, culture, and administration. Without any explanation or justification, following obediently the current doctrines of racial division, Le Corbusier "set aside for Europeans" the Residential City on the amphitheatric slope, and he assigned a "separate city for the indigenous population."

Thus, Le Corbusier's Nemours plan clearly obeyed the principles of colonial rule. Did he agree with them? Was he blind to them? Did he think that society would benefit in a general sense from the implementation of his plan even if some individuals would benefit more than others would? In the text of the plan, it is stated that "the most recent advances in architecture and city planning can be put to work" for "both residential zones." Was this an apology? What confuses the issue even more is the fact that although the Residential City was not intended for the "indigenes," he proudly called it the

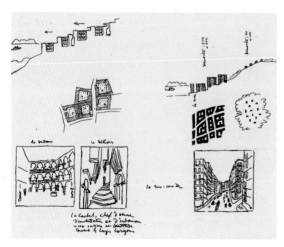

Sketches comparing Arabic to European Urbanism

The Naval Zone at Algiers, 1938–1942: sketches showing the business district in relation to the kasbah and skyscraper

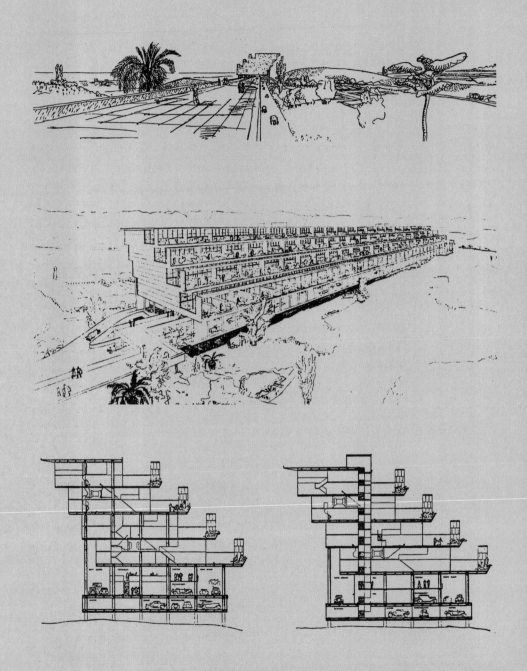

Durand Housing Estate, Oued-Ouchaia, Algiers, 1933

"new Casbah of Algiers, a Casbah of modern times, made out of steel and cement." Reciprocally, he declared repeatedly that the Casbah was more advanced than European colonial architecture, the architecture whose social and political values he had always before accepted as superior.

In addition to the large-scale urbanistic projects, Le Corbusier worked on a number of building projects. However, even there he was preoccupied with how these individual schemes as prototypical units that could be multiplied, fitting into a vaster fabric, and aimed at conserving the character and quality of the Mediterranean landscape that was already in danger due to urbanization and industrial and engineering infrastructure decvelopment. The **Appartements for Rent** project of 1933 was a prototype for buildings at the ledge of the Algiers cliffs. To adapt to the topography and to minimize circulation, the entrance was placed in the middle of the volume. The tower offered high-density housing with magnificent views of the Mediterranean, yet disturbed only minimally the contours of the landscape. Similarly, the **Durand Housing Estate** project, designed in 1933–1934, provided concentrated housing for 300 families in the midst of a splendid vineyard. Although it was basically a housing block, Le Corbusier transformed it into a hanging garden estate by setting back each individual floor and providing a terrace for each apartment. Given the attractiveness of the surrounding views and the mildness of the climate, he offered an attractive alternative for the middle-class residents of Algiers in search of a home with outdoor private space. Its high-density land occupation and the application of the high *pilotis* were Le Corbusier's early warning and response to the undoing of the Mediterranean landscape already visible at that time.

Villa in Carthage, North Africa

Partially because of the need to generate income and partially because of his curiosity to explore, rather than to experiment with, new possibilities in the midst of these gigantic, complex projects, Le Corbusier undertook a number of private residences. What is common in all these projects was his wish to work with local constraints, potentials, and values – in short, designing special cases rather than developing universal rules. In fact, he explored only one region, the Mediterranean. Thus, common to all these projects was their engagement with Mediterranean materials, climate, and local building prototypes. In contrast to the villas of the previous decade, these private houses do not show the research rigor and laboratory control that led the major conclusions of the previous decade.

The earliest project in this series of investigations in a renewed regionalism was the 1930 **house for M. Errazuris** in Chile. Le Corbusier saw the region of Chile through the lens of the Mediterranean. He claimed that these two distant parts of the world resembled each other so much that a contemporary local Chilean architecture could use Mediterranean knowledge. The plan of the building reflected a modern way of living while the Chilean environment suggested combining the use of local materials and centuries-old Mediterranean methods of construction and the stoa prototype for the plan scheme. If the villa did not have enormous influence in Chile, its impact in Mediterranean architecture after World War II was most significant.

A similar approach was applied in 1928 for the **Villa Hélène de Mandrot.** Hélène de Mandrot was an admirer of architecture. Sympathetic to Le Corbusier's insult with the Palace of the League of

Villa Errazuriz, Chile 1930 (left and opposite page)

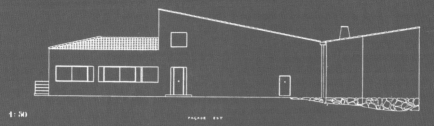

1 : 50

FAÇADE EST

Façade sur la montagne

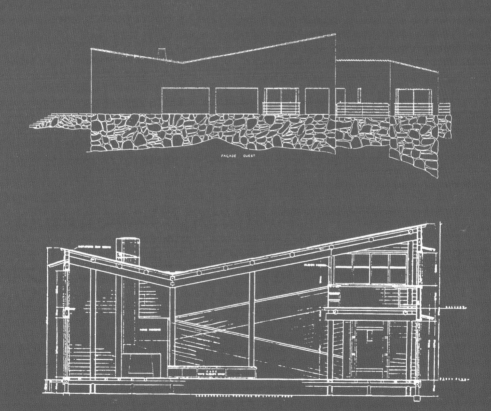

FAÇADE OUEST

Nations, she offered her Château of Sarraz, in the Canton of Vaud in Switzerland, for a preparatory meeting of the Congress of Modern Architecture. Impressed further by Le Corbusier, she commissioned him to design a vacation house for her in Le Pradet, near Toulon, France, in 1932. There, Le Corbusier applied his new *regionalist* framework. The materials were a combination of regional stone, used for the vertical bearing elements, and reinforced concrete, for the horizontal flat roof, that were also drawn from the precedents of Mediterranean cubic structures. The scheme was also recruited from a Mediterranean prototype, the stoa. As in peasant houses, constructed by additions, the sequence of spaces was linear, or "paratactic." There were no winding paths of a *promenade architectural*. Le Corbusier handled the relation between built volume and outside through simple, "stoac" means. Abandoning his own dogma of the horizontal continuous window, he used a variety of openings, offering a variety of frames to the landscape. Also in the spirit of Mediterranean vernacular structures, he added next to the built volume a bare terrace, open to the panorama of the surroundings. Unfortunately, Le Corbusier was once more a victim of self-deception. The rustic, regional materials combined with modern materials and details did not behave as Le Corbusier expected them to do. Water penetrated the building from every side, making the house uninhabitable and requiring expensive repairs. Nonetheless, Villa Mandrot, like the house of M. Errazuris in Chile, was considered a most influential prototype in post–World War II Mediterranean architecture.

Several times Le Corbusier appeared to have acted adventurously, irresponsibly, or naïvely concerning technical matters. He showed a narcissistic attitude in relation to how materials were to behave and a callous indifference to his clients if their behavior turned out to be different from what he desired. Yet, people attracted by the force of his beliefs and the fire of his visions continued to trust him. Typical was the case of the contractor of the Cité de Refuge, Albin Peyron. The Cité, as with Villa Mandrot, had posed major technical problems, yet in 1935, Peyron commissioned Le Corbusier to design his daughter's house, the **Villa le Sextant**, located in La Palmyre-Les Mathes, Charente-Maritime, France. As Peyron stated in a letter to Le Corbusier, this was not a house for weekend outings, parties, or cultural happenings. It was a limited-budget, ordinary, durable vacation home for a contractor's daughter. The low budget did not allow importing building materials from Paris or hiring specialized labor to construct in what had become the usual, "chic" Le Corbusier manner. There was not even enough money for Le Corbusier to travel to the site from Paris. But Le Corbusier accepted the challenge. He designed a truly *regional* house, respecting all the prerequisites of his client. He used photographic documentation of the site. He circumscribed his scheme within the limits and opportunities of what was locally accessible. As with Villa Mandrot, local stone was used for the walls, but this time local traditions were applied to make them waterproof, and this time the stone was combined with wood and applied for an inclined roof. Similarly, all construction details were selected with the consideration that local builders, without much supervision, could easily apply them. Great care was taken to control the quality of the microclimate of the villa by simply applying the most natural, traditional means – strategic placement of walls and openings for shading and ventilation – all taking into consideration the local microclimate. The spatial scheme was also similar to Villa Mandrot in that the Villa le Sextant used the Mediterranean stoa prototype. This time, all functional, technical, and financial matters went as planned and the client was grateful to Le Corbusier.

Villa le Sextant, Mathes, France, 1935

Rethinking the regional and the modern as complementary approaches within a larger framework of design theory, during the early part of the 1930s, Le Corbusier did not prohibit himself from dealing with other generic problems such as the redefinition of roofs. As we have seen, by the end of the 1920s, he had invented what he called in the beginning simply the solarium, a new element that combined the Mediterranean precedent of the small open court with the deck of a vessel. He subsequently applied his invention in most of his villas and in projects of collective housing. In 1933 he tried it himself in a pilot project. He conceived his own home and workplace, his studio of "patient research," as he called it, on the top of an apartment house he designed, the Molitor, in Paris. He covered the building on both east and west sides with glass "with no protection against the sun." Thus it was here that the idea of the "brise-soleil was invented."

A similar case was the design in 1930 of the top two floors of a Parisian apartment house at Champs-Elysées for **Charles de Beistégui**, a rich man who wanted a second residence in the heart of the crowded metropolis for his entertainment. As he had with his own penthouse, Le Corbusier explored the idiosyncratic parameters of the specific program to pursue his patient research concerning the development of general rules and prototypes, at the same time giving shape to a new, unique object. This product, however, amounted to a most eccentric interpretation of the general problem. Exploring the control of light and glare was not as important here as the exploitation of the opportunities to display the surrounding urban landscape. As with Palladio's Villa Rotonda and Le Corbusier's own Villa Savoye, the objective of the project was to design a place for high-class social diversion where

Penthouse Apartment for Charles
de Beistégui, Champs-Elysées,
Paris, 1930: roof terrace, courtesy
Lucien Herve

distant vistas and close encounters would play an equally important role. Le Corbusier openly declared that the project interested him because it presented a "program vedette," a "star program" for which he could supply what M. Peyron had called a "Le Corbusier chic" artifact. He wanted to offer to his client and his guests in the middle of the city "the sensation of a liner in the ocean." The plan was to supply the strange sense of repose and festivity, of distant views and mingling, all under the sky in a way that one had only up to that moment found on the deck of transatlantic luxury liners. Once more, even in this cramped space, a scenario of movement was the basic means to organize space. As one circulated, descending/ascending through a suspended spiral stair, one experienced on one hand the different dispositions of people engaged in social intercourse, and on the other the different aspects of the Parisian panorama. Once inside, projections and a periscope – camouflaged on the terrace as a liner's ventilator – brought in the thrill of the city's skyline. The extreme bizarreness of the fabricated experience suggests a surrealist influence.

Faithful to his habit, Le Corbusier once more overspent. The cost of the project tripled – the contractor, though, invited Le Corbusier to work with him for other projects that followed. Such personal connections played a most important role in Le Corbusier's work. He was a master in knitting networks of relatives, compatriots, and trusted acquaintances to advance ideas, publications, and commissions. However, the mental memory lines of precedents and the networks of concepts and models have been more significant to determine his design explorations. It was the spatial intelligence with which he was endowed the habit of the mind that he acquired by training himself throughhis early art school years

Penthouse Apartment for Charles de Beistégui: interior staircase, courtesy Lucien Herve

Penthouse Apartment for Charles de
Beistégui: roof terrace and periscope,
courtesy Lucien Herve

that made him a master of reinvention and recombination of previous artifacts and natural objects. Certainly, next to that were the socioeconomic situation and the constraints of the cultural-political settings. One may easily link the eccentric, the absurd, and the conspicuous consumption character of the Beistégui roof villa to what Léon Blum called in his 1945 manifesto *A l'Échele Humaine*, the "illusion of prosperity," the "*jouissance facile*," the fun-and-games character of the times. The aura of spectacle and illusion and the atmosphere of casual encounter predominate in the scheme, resembling the epochal 1930s films of Jean Renoir. The roof villa can be seen as a machine for sustaining – to quote historian Marc Bloch – the "absence of realism"; the "alchemist mentality;" the deceit and the corruption that led to the Stavisky affair, which had occurred two years after the completion of the Beistégui roof villa; and finally to the collapse of the liberal European institutions by the end of the 1930s. One may also link Le Corbusier's turn to regional investigations during the 1930s to the rise of the right and its attacks against modern architecture and its ideas about mechanization and what we now call "globalism." In this case, Le Corbusier was not trying to change his approach to architecture in self-defense. Rather, he was trying to demonstrate that there was no inherent contradiction between the search for industrialization, universal rules, international collaboration, and regional needs and opportunities.

While construction was coming to completion in the Arcadian Villa le Sextant, the mood in France and in the rest of Europe was drastically changing. There would be immediate repercussions for the work with which Le Corbusier was involved.

"Between the sum of errors and the dawn of renewal"   **CHAPTER 04**

I

During the second part of the 1930s, the political scene in France and all of Europe became increasingly intense, radical, and ultimately brutal. The polarization of the 1930s pressed intellectuals and artists to choose between being revolutionaries or bourgeois capitalists. The impact these events had on Le Corbusier was mixed. Whether dealing with spatial compositional or with functional morphological problems, Le Corbusier appeared to be pursuing his design explorations following their own internal logic. In 1925, having been attacked by *L'Humanité* for his 1922 Salon d'Automne exhibition, Le Corbusier tried to make clear where he stood politically. In his book *Urbanism*, he declared that a good city plan had to do with qualities such as geometry, light, circulation, economy, and health, good things in themselves that did not need to be attached to special facilities called "House of the People" or "Seat of the Labor Union." On the other hand, he reminded his critics, in order to carry out his Plan Voisin, it would be necessary to expropriate the whole center of Paris, an act that was clearly political as it would effect private property. Still, he insisted, he was operating on the technical rather than the political level. "I am an architect," he avowed, and he stated he could not behave like a politician. He insisted that his studies were "addressed neither to the capitalist society nor to the 3rd International." He concluded the book by declaring that one does not "make a revolution revolutionizing. One makes a revolution by producing solutions." This was a much more reflective and far-reaching statement than his much-quoted 1923 statement, "Architecture or revolution." It was resolved that "revolution can be avoided."

Not only the left was suspicious of the meaning of his work, but the extreme right was almost paranoid about him, as they were about most modern architects. We have already discussed the slandering of his Swiss pavilion in the Swiss press. Also in Switzerland, a 1931 pamphlet under the formidable title *The Trojan Horse of Bolshevism* by Sengers, pointed the finger at Le Corbusier as a person advancing dangerous ideas in conspiracy with the "Jews, the free-masons" and the Soviets, who "supplied him with orders." Equally accusatory was a series of articles in the *Figaro* by Camille Mauclair. Mauclair talked about the dangers of Le Corbusier's "panbetonizm" (making the whole world out of concrete), distraction from tradition, and his links with the "communist cell of La Sarraz" and with "Mammon, the god of capitalism."

The political developments affected the type of projects with which Le Corbusier was involved. In 1936 the Popular Front, an anti-fascist coalition of left-wing parties, won the elections and formed a government in France. After this victory, the leading leftist politician, Paul Vaillant-Couturier, the editor of *L'Humanité,* approached Le Corbusier to apologize for the attacks he received in the pages of his paper. Le Corbusier responded by saying that to his "view there is only one way the Popular Front can demonstrate that something new was occurring in the field of social justice. It is to construct immediately in Paris housing that would reflect the latest developments in modern techniques and offer it to the people." He subsequently joined him in the historical May 24, 1936 anti-fascist rally composed of 600,000 delegates including Louis Aragon and other luminaries of the left. By 1937, the Popular Front

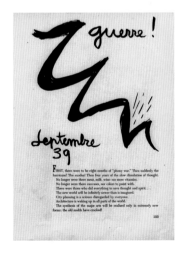

Illustration from *New World of Space* (1948)

was out of the government and Vaillant-Couturier was dead. A committee to honor his memory (which included Jean Renoir among others) decided to erect a monument to his memory. Two years later, after a competition, Le Corbusier was selected to build the monument. Le Corbusier's proposal was beyond the budget and the project was never built. In his *Œuvre*, Le Corbusier boasted that the design was included in an exhibition organized by the Museum of Modern Art (MOMA) to travel throughout the United States on the theme of war memorials in 1945.

The site for the monument was at the corner of the Fontainebleau route and the boulevard Maxime-Gorki, at Villejuif (the southern suburb of Paris), where Vaillant-Couturier was the major. Le Corbusier conceived the scheme as an object to be seen in movement, and this is of particular historical importance because it made the project one of the first "highway" works of architecture. It explained the spatial composition of the scheme and the hierarchy of scales applied. The immense size and the bareness of the forms, the violent encounter between the vertical wall and the long half-cantilevered, prismatic volume extending horizontally, like a figure of a stretched arm coming out of a torso, were to be read from a very long distance. Approaching the intersection, the driver would recognize fragments of the figure of an orator, an open hand gesturing out towards the sky, a head with the mouth shouting, and an open book. Le Corbusier envisaged that the memorial would be illuminated at night. Together, with the monument to the victims of the March 1920 demonstration by Walter Gropius and the Karl Liebknecht-Rosa Luxemburg monument by Mies van der Rohe, Le Corbusier's – by far the most moving, complex, and most architectural – is one of the products of political art of the twentieth-

Projected Monument to Paul Vaillant, Villejuif, France, 1937

century left. Despite the fact that Vaillant-Couturier was not a martyr, the character of the composition was sublime, protesting, and tragic. Although no direct references can be made to any of the images, the figure's shouting mouth and the outstretched hand were obviously influenced by Picasso's *Guernica*. *Guernica* in fact was exhibited next to Le Corbusier's pavilion in the 1937 *Exposition Internationale des Arts et des Techniques* in the Spanish Pavilion designed by Luis Lacasa and a Catalan admirer of Le Corbusier, Jose Luis Sert, who would later become dean at the Harvard Graduate School of Design.

The 1937 *Exposition Internationale* was another project under the Popular Front government. The plans for the exhibition and Le Corbusier's efforts to be part of them have a longer history. Since 1855, Paris had been the site of a series of major international expositions; one of them was the 1925 *Exposition des Arts Décoratifs*, for which Le Corbusier designed his Pavillon de L'Esprit Nouveau. The idea for a new exposition came up again in 1929. In 1932 Le Corbusier proposed as its subject an International Exhibition of Housing, or more exactly Habitation, a real ambitious large-scale project demonstrating the new approaches to urbanism. The theme did not appeal to the conservative organizers of the event. Two years later, an insistent Le Corbusier proposed a scaled-down version of the idea, an exhibition linked with the investigations of CIAM, with Housing and Leisure as a central theme. This idea was received better, but finally it was not accepted. A third project was proposed on the theme of the Museum of Unlimited Growth. Le Corbusier reworked previous schemes of a spiral space expanding without end. The idea was praised by a sympathetic administration that had been appointed by the Popular Front. It was called prophetic but also problematic and ultimately not so

relevant. Finally, after a decade of discussions and debates, Le Corbusier was commissioned to design the **Pavillion du Temps-Nouveaux** ("Pavilion of New Times") in the framework of the theme *Exposition Internationale des Arts et des Techniques dans la vie Moderne* in 1937. He designed a structure covering 15,000 meters of space using canvas held by cable and metallic frame columns. The idea was that this tentlike pavilion could be easily demountable to be able to travel around, as constructivists did with their exhibitions in the U.S.S.R. The subject was again Le Corbusier's ideas about the city and, more precisely, a proposal for the *Plan of Paris '37*. As in the pavilion for the L'Esprit Nouveau, Le Corbusier used large panoramic panels with graphics or photomontages, models, and dioramas.

While Le Corbusier in 1934 was trying to convince the authorities of the exposition with his idea for an urban scheme and the theme of Housing and Leisure, a group of young artists who collectively went by the name Young '37, together with his associate interior designer Charlotte Perriand, conceived a parallel idea. The initiator was Le Corbusier's cousin and collaborator Pierre Jeanneret, who after a visit to a feast organized by *L'Humanité* thought of a national center dedicated to popular celebrations. Nothing came from this idea at that time, but Le Corbusier quickly adopted it. The result was a proposal to the Popular Front in 1937 for a gigantic **Stadium for 100,000 people** for Paris. Although the complex included facilities for sports, including football, swimming, tennis, and bicycling, it was conceived of as more than just an athletic center. Le Corbusier tried to facilitate shows by providing a colossal film screen and an equally gigantic stage adaptable in size and shape to fit all types of performances of music, theater, dance, circus spectacles, and mass happenings. An enormous

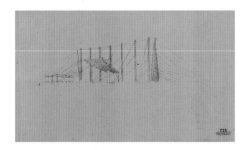 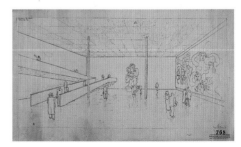

100,000 Seat Stadium, Bois de
Vincennes, Paris, France 1937
(above); Pavillion du Temps-Nouveaux,
Paris, France, 1937: conceptual
sketches (opposite page)

folding tent suspended from a huge inclined mast protected the whole amphitheater in case of bad weather. The whole complex, the auditorium and stage, could become one united and uniting space when popular feasts were taking place. It was as if Le Corbusier was responding to the text of the great historian Marc Bloch in his *The Strange Defeat*, which Bloch wrote clandestinely three years before being executed by the Nazis. Bloch was reflecting on the deep problems France faced before the war that ultimately led to French defeat. He remarked that France was deprived of any true popular feasts. This neglect by all governments caused a deprivation of collective enthusiasm and a mood of hopelessness and despair. Bloch stressed that such democratic popular festivals were the contrary of the totalitarian mass rallies. Their objective would be to bring about a sense of joy in life and a belief in doing things together. Le Corbusier responded in kind, and his scheme was a reaction to what the Nazis had generously provided the year before, the Albert Speer Zeppelin Field, accommodating 240,000 participants and 150 searchlights for night rallies and the Werner March Olympic Grounds and Stadium for 100,000 spectators.

II

On June 14, 1940, the German army entered Paris. Le Corbusier closed down his studio in Rue de Sévre and like the French government and many Parisians, he and his wife left Paris for the Pyrenees. In July of the same year, the Vichy government was set up. Soon after, in October, the government passed a decree prohibiting French citizens of Jewish origin to work for the state. By the end of the year, the Vichy government passed the first law concerning the status of practicing architects. A

ministerial decision was passed permitting three people without diplomas to practice; one of them was Le Corbusier, another was Le Corbusier's old mentor Auguste Perret. Before long, in January 1941, Le Corbusier was invited by the government to come to Vichy. By then his cousin and collaborator Pierre Jeanneret was working underground as a member of the resistance. The move was clever from the side of the gerontocratic government, as Marc Bloch characterized it. Le Corbusier accepted to collaborate with Jeanneret and in May, a decree signed by General Pétain himself appointed him chief of the state housing organization. This was not the first time Le Corbusier tried to work with the highest authorities. He appealed to Mussolini and he wrote several letters to Léon Blum with concrete proposals to which he received no answer. Neither was it the first time Le Corbusier had shown indifference to totalitarian regimes. During the beginning of the Stalinist repression, without a word of criticism of the regime or any sign of compassion for its victims, he continued to work with the government. Even when his books were returned by the Soviet state bookshops as unwanted material and his own friends started to have difficulties with the authorities, he kept on seeking projects in the U.S.S.R. Pétain's offer was the closest he would ever be to bureaucratic power and to a totalitarian authority. In fact, it was not as close as it first appeared, nor did it last very long.

In June 1941, Le Corbusier flew to Algiers. He returned again to Algiers in 1942 to continue with his study of the plan of the city of Algiers. Soon he had ready what he called no more an urban but a **Master Plan**. The plan epitomized his previous researches – it included the city, its region, the hinterland, and it extended to Paris. In it Le Corbusier tried to grasp the supercity emerging out of the

Sketch for an automobile, 1936

intercity networks of circulation. He had originally sketched the idea in South America, in his December 21, 1929 lecture in Estuary of the Gironde entitled "The World City." It was researched in depth later during the war. The war did not seem to have influenced this vision. On the contrary, it appeared that it confirmed Le Corbusier's ideas about mass movement, international operations, and technological might. This final project focused on "native" institutions and the Marine quarter. The area previously designated for a business center became a Muslim center, and the business center moved to the "European Town." The conservation of the Casbah became an essential component of the plan. As opposed to the European colonial "contribution" (Le Corbusier held a low opinion of it and saw no future there), he considered the Casbah a quality environment that had to be preserved. The shift in his plan giving priority to the facilities for native Algerians probably reflected the advancement of the western army of the Allied Forces in Northern Africa and the rising power of the local movements.

The most elaborate part of the project was the architecture of the individual buildings, in particular a hotel skyscraper. Its rectangular form was deduced by "rational" analysis as opposed to American prewar analysis that Le Corbusier felt was shaped by formal, historicist considerations. The facade was the most important contribution of the scheme and would later have a tremendous influence on postwar architecture. As opposed to the universal idea of the glass curtain wall, which had already been developed by Le Corbusier, the **Algiers Marine skyscraper** facade was regionalist. Given the impact of the Mediterranean sun, Le Corbusier, elaborating on the brise-soleil, which had been developed for the Ministry of Brazil, advanced an elaborate kind of colossal Southern Italian shutter,

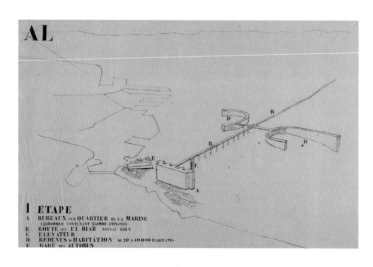

covering the front of the whole building. It consisted of "vertical and horizontal fins," fixed or adjustable. Le Corbusier had calculated them to "give shade after a certain date … from the latitude of the site." The dimensions of the grid formed by the "fins" varied according to the uses behind it giving the facade an intricate pattern. Further on, they were proportioned to "achieve harmony," according to the prolpulsion system of the Golden Section. The colonial regime did not appear to have been moved by any of these proposals. Le Corbusier was a man agitating for modern ideas in the midst of retrenching conservatism. He appeared even as a possible professional competitor. Last but not least there were serious rumors, articles in the press, and a reprint of the 1931 *The Trojan Horse of Bolshevism*, reiterating the rumors that he was a communist with strong ties to Jewish conspirators.

Finally, Le Corbusier understood that there was no hope for commissions and that he was persona non grata in Algiers. Once he realized this, he concentrated his activities in Paris for the last two years of the war. There he took part in numerous meetings with groups working on the reorganization of a postwar France. Preparing for the day of the liberation, he opened again his office and tried to gather a younger generation of collaborators. He worked harder toward a flexible universal proportioning system, hoping to restore harmony and order to a world that needed it very much. That system would become known as the Modulor.

Paris was liberated on Saturday, August 19, 1944. On May 8, 1945, it celebrated the end of the war in la Place de la Concorde. For Le Corbusier, the celebration was a "proof of urbanism."

Project from A, B, C, and H, Algiers: elevated highway and sea-scrapers

Huts, Bottleracks, and Liners   **CHAPTER** 05

Paris was liberated on August 19, 1944. Three months later, the retreating Germans, still on French territory, demolished half of the city of Saint-Dié, in Vosges, and 10,500 people were left homeless. (That was the second time the city was destroyed; the first was by fire in the middle of the eighteenth century. Rebuilt immediately after the fire, it became an industrial town with a high-quality historical center.) Le Corbusier, excluded from all French government committees and associations, was in 1944 working privately on the development of the Modulor. However, at the beginning of 1945, Jean-Jacques Duval, a young entrepreneur and friend of Le Corbusier, invited him, on behalf of the city's Popular Association of War Victims – a private organization of proprietors – to provide architectural advice for the devastated city. Le Corbusier worked first on temporary housing, a subject he had thought about since World War I. Before long, he was officially appointed to provide a plan for the reconstruction of the devastated **Saint-Dié** (1945–1946). Clearly, this was a unique opportunity to present the new ideas of modern architecture. Before the war, modern architectural ideas had had a provocative, utopian character; by 1945 they had become pertinent and urgent.

Le Corbusier tried to include in the plan his urbanistic ideas as they had crystalized in the compelling principle-based *Charte d'Athenes,* which he had published during the occupation in 1942. He therefore proposed high-rise apartments implanted in a patchwork of parks and playfields and enmeshed in a hierarchy of paths and roads. In contrast to this plan, Jacques André, the official planner of Saint-Dié and an admirer of Le Corbusier, adopted in his recommendation the original geometry and the existing building types of the plan of Duc de Lorraine. Nonetheless, the Popular Association of War

Plan for the reconstruction of Saint-Dié, France (1945–1946 (51)): plan and perspective

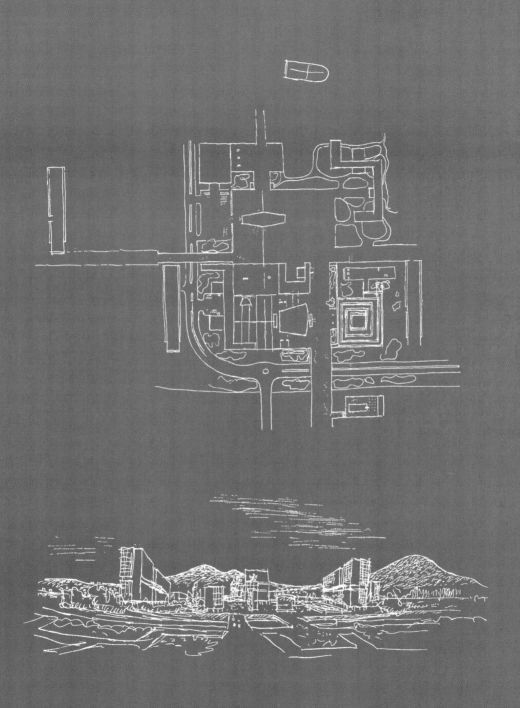

Victims, which was numerous in membership and held left-wing political beliefs, rejected both proposals and opted for a faithful reconstruction. Following his "physiocratic" habit, Le Corbusier by-passed the objections of the local users and tried to appeal to the higher benevolent authority, the heads of the left-wing union CGT. He even pursued his prewar Popular Front and old New Times connections to help him. However, he did not realize that the postwar times were different. All these efforts produced the opposite results. They distanced him further from the people of the town, whose desire for empowerment and appropriation of their living environment Le Corbusier had under-estimated. Allowing no room for dialogue and participation and without quitting the job, Le Corbusier left behind Saint-Dié and its worrying inhabitants. By December 1945, he was sailing for New York on the Liberty ship *Vernon*.

The voyage on the *Vernon* was marked by stormy weather. Instead of taking seven to nine days to cross the ocean, as was customary at that time, it took nineteen. "We slept in dormitories," Le Corbusier wrote, "the cabins being occupied by the crew." He carried in his pocket an aluminum Kodak film box containing the tape measure of the proportioning system that would become the Modulor, his pre-occupation at that moment. In a cabin that he was allowed to use from 8 a.m. to noon and 8 p.m. to midnight in the evening, as he recounted the story in the first volume of the Modulor (published 1950), he overcame all the difficulties and resolved the system. In January 1946, before his return, the municipal council of Saint-Dié voted definitively against Le Corbusier's project.

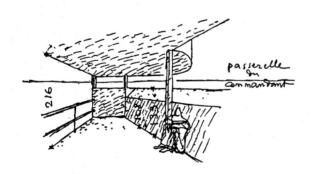

Drawing showing dimensions of the ship *Liberty*, 1945 (left); Modulor Man, 1950 (opposite page)

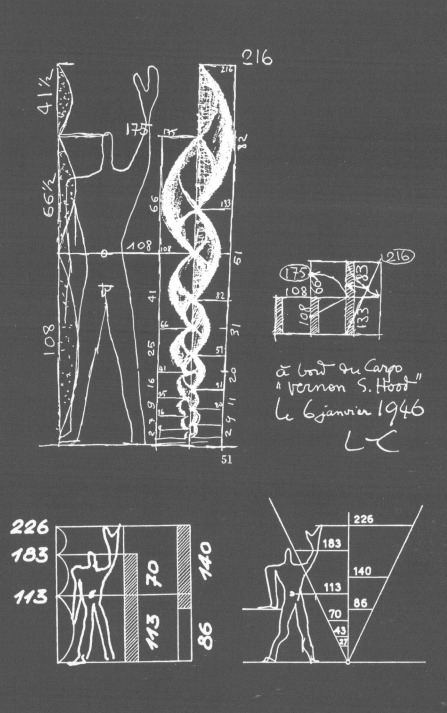

216

41½

175   135

66½

108   108

108

66

51

82

133

82

31

51

20

51

27

2726

à bord du Cargo
« Vernon S. Hood »
Le 6 janvier 1946
LC

175   108   99   83   216
108   133

226

183

113

70

140

113   86

226

183

140

113

86

70

43

27

As Le Corbusier narrated in his *Œuvre Complète*, his plan for Saint-Dié was "unanimously rejected by the upper, middle, and lower classes." People of the left rejected it because they wanted their houses made in the local stone of the Vosges region – something Le Corbusier would not have objected to in the 1930s, as we have seen. They did so despite the fact that the Architects National Front (FNA), a national left-wing organization, had explicitly warned against the attachment to traditional materials for reconstruction and suggested that more innovative techniques be accepted. They rejected it also because Le Corbusier had a "monopoly" in the conception of the project while the inhabitants played no role. Last but not least, they disapproved of the idea that the reconstruction of their town was categorized as a "pilot project." Likewise, the French Confederation of Christian Workers rejected Le Corbusier's plan. They felt that his high-rise apartments would scatter families and that his planning ideas were "collectivist," yet at the same time favoring "the housing trusts" for "making profit." This time Le Corbusier could not blame academic architects and conservative authorities for the rejection of his proposals. The fate of another Le Corbusier reconstruction project of the same period, La Rochelle–La Pallice, was similar.

The causes of Le Corbusier's failure became clearer in view of a contemporary reconstruction plan for a town of the same scale, Mauberge. André Lurçat, the architect of that project, advocated the same ideas of modern architecture as Le Corbusier and was a member of CIAM, but he succeeded in building his project with the complete support of its inhabitants. In stark contrast to Le Corbusier, Lurçat understood the changes that had occurred in the attitudes and expectations of the people during the

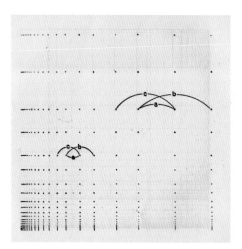

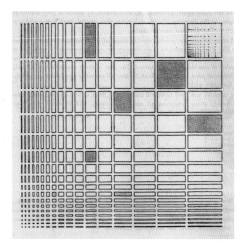

war. The shock of the defeat, the trauma of the occupation, and the anger at the Vichy regime contributed to an antiauthoritarian spirit and to the rise of the importance of human rights. This had major implications in every walk of life. Contrary to Le Corbusier, in the early 1930s, Lurçat already considered dialogue with the users as an integral part of the planning and design process. For Mauberge, he established regular procedures for meeting and exchanging ideas during which, step by step, the final plan emerged. That sustained the adoption of spatial formal and operational innovations and, as André Chastel wrote in *Le Monde* in 1947, enhanced the radical redistribution of property and new forms of collective property.

In less than half a year, Le Corbusier was back in the United States. With a Soviet architect – Nikolai Bassov, the architect who had won the competition of the Palace of the Soviets – he circled Nelson Rockefeller's residence in New York State in a plane chartered by the Rockefellers. The object of the ride – the pilot suspected that it had to do with spying – was to study possible sites for the **Headquarters of the United Nations**, the "sequel" to the prewar Geneva institution for which Le Corbusier did not win the commission, although he had won the competition. Le Corbusier, involved from the beginning in the development of the United Nations project, was also involved with the selection of the site and with the writing of a special report produced by the French about the building program. There, he made a strong point that the future scheme had not only to serve the practical needs of the organization but also to demonstrate a new way of life. Among other objectives, he stated that the UN facility had "to eliminate daily long distance transportation between … work … dwelling … recreation,"

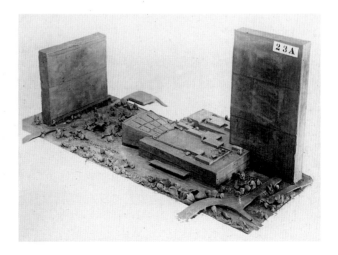

Sketches from Modulor
(opposite page); Headquarters
of the United Nations, New York,
New York, 1947 (right)

to "organize home to free [their] housewives of harassing toils," to "make intellectual development available to all," and to "exclude egoism and bring forth values of individuals and community."

The process of deciding on all the complex issues related to the UN project had very little to do with the naïve prewar machinations of the palace in Geneva. Postwar political realities demanded a transparent, democratic process, and Trygve Lie, the first UN secretary-general, was determined to achieve it. Thus, he wanted to appoint an international board of design. Wallis K. Harrison became director of planning and chairman of this board that, in addition to Le Corbusier, included Oscar Niemeyer, Robert Moses, and Matthew Novicki, as special design consultant. Given the number of participating nations, the political significance that the United Nations assumed at that moment, and the economic interests associated with the location and the operation of the organization, the design-by-committee approach was an invitation to trouble rather than the "shortcut" alternative of a competition.

Le Corbusier was among people who respected his ideas but were not necessarily ready to accept his proposals in their entirety or himself as the chief architect of the complex. Le Corbusier was seen as a troublemaker, lacking pragmatism and even management experience for a project of this scale and importance. In addition, behind the decision for the architecture of the building, there were innumerable interests, political as well as private and financial. The location of the project especially had serious political implications and repercussions on real estate values. Le Corbusier did not appear to be the right person to maneuver through all that.

Proposal for the Urbanization of
La Rochelle-Palace, 1945–1946

From the formal or functional point of view, Le Corbusier's UN project was not a significant one. He proposed a standard division of functions, assigning administrative operations to office cells stacked vertically in a high-density prismatic slab that resembled his Ministry of Education and Public Health in Rio de Janeiro. Despite the fact that Le Corbusier was reported to have declared that "the Assembly is the king," by its sheer size the dominant component in the scheme was the characteristic slab in the assembly hall. It is significant in the history of tall buildings in New York City as the first non-pyramidal, "Cartesian" skyscraper. Its impact on the configuration of Manhattan lasted for more than two decades. As political intrigue, real-estate machination, and mixture of both, it is a unique case in history.

It was in 1945 – as the Allied Armies were approaching Berlin – that Le Corbusier had been asked by Raoul Dautry, the first postwar minister of reconstruction in France, to design a large residential unit. The project was to be financed directly by the state without any zoning restrictions. The site was not specified in the beginning. Four different locations were considered, all to be placed in "the heart of the Homeric landscape" of Marseilles, "the city he loved," as Le Corbusier had declared. Le Corbusier did not waste time in starting, but it took ten successive governments and seven different ministers of reconstruction for it to be completed. The acceptance of Le Corbusier's scheme by the French bureaucrats and the government was not immediate. André Wogenscky, one of Le Corbusier's close collaborators, wrote of the "countless meetings, discussions, and formalities" involving the "authorities," "persons and organizations" who because of "routine and stupidity," lack of understanding of the project, or "jealousy and spitefulness" almost wrecked the realization of the project.

Unité d'Habitation, Marseille,
France, 1952: model

The first stone of **Unité d'Habitation, Marseille**, as the project came to be known, was laid on October 14, 1949. The building was finished and handed over to Eugène Claudius-Petit, then the minister of reconstruction and town planning, by Le Corbusier on October 14, 1952.

One of Le Corbusier's very first steps was to put together a team of experts and assistants to collaborate in the development of the scheme and work out every detail of the project. Without doubt, as we have seen up to now, Le Corbusier was a self-centered person. He perceived and presented himself as lonely explorer, pioneer, and martyr. Indeed, his "patient research" was recited in the *Œuvre Complète* as an internal stream of investigations carrying with it experiences, passing through memory and driven by desires, aspirations, and incorporated values toward the discoveries of the future. He was always solitary, yet never alone. Earlier in his life, he was in constant dialogue with a series of relatives, mentors, and confidants, and finally clients, collaborators and assistants. Clients such as Édouard Trouin (see Chapter 6) played a very significant role (almost like coworkers) in the conception of a project. As Wogenscky wrote, despite Le Corbusier's "prima donna" public appearances, far from generating ideas in isolation, he "had always been convinced of the need for the architect to collaborate with all the technicians starting with the elaboration of the very first draft." The role of Charlotte Perriand, not to mention his formal partner and relative Pierre Jeanneret, was most significant for the development of several major projects. Le Corbusier sensed that the Unité was going to become a most important project and he tried from the outset to secure maximum support for it. Thus, he rushed to assemble the Atelier des Bâtisseurs, known as ATBAT, that became dedicated to the creation of the Unité. It was a workshop

Unité d'Habitation: roof terrace, photograph by Lucien Herve

divided into four sections, made up of "homogeneous" teams: administrative, managerial, technical, and architectural. Le Corbusier realized very soon that interaction between the various specialists was taking place mostly after the design phase, with negative repercussions. For this reason he appointed autonomous heads for each section, reserving for himself the direction of the architectural one only. Among the specialists was Vladimir Bodiansky, an aircraft desinger, for engineering and of course Charlotte Perriand for interior design.

For a freestanding building for housing, a single "box of homes," as Le Corbusier called it, the Unité d'Habitation was huge by contemporary standards. The block was 165 meters long, 56 meters high, and 24 meters deep, standing on massive *pilotis* in the midst of a large park area of 3.5 hectares (3.5 x 2.47 acres), its main elevations facing east and west. The massive *pilotis* contained the service pipes. Resting on them were technical installations. The free area underneath it was used for circulation and parking, as well as the entrance, elevators, and janitor's closet. Underneath the first floor were the air conditioning plant, elevator machinery, and diesel generators. The project consisted of eighteen floors, 337 dwellings varying in twenty-three different types for 1,500 to 1,700 inhabitants, ranging from bachelor to family-size apartments for families with up to eight children. The apartments were distributed in pairs of three floors; they could be accessed by only five corridors, "interior roads," one on every third floor.

Unité d'Habitation: interior streets (above) and facade detail (opposite page), photographs by Michael Levin

An apartment contained two floors connected with an interior staircase. The day room, 4.80 meters tall, extended over two floors. A large window of 3.66 x 4.80 meters allowed a full view of the landscape. The kitchen contained a four-plate electric range with oven, a double sink with automatic garbage disposal, a refrigerator, and a worktable. It was air-conditioned by the central system. The sound insulation consisted of lead sheets between the separating walls of the apartments.

Along the interior road on levels 7 and 8 rested a shopping center, containing fish, butcher, milk, and fruit and vegetable shops, as well as a bakery, a liquor store, and a drugstore. Furthermore, there was a laundry and cleaning service, pharmacy, barbershop, and a post office. Along the same corridor, there was a provision for a hotel accommodation, a snack bar, and a restaurant. Finally, there was a catering service to the apartments, a dream of Le Corbusier's since the 1920s.

The final floor accommodated a kindergarten and a nursery, from which a ramp led to a roof-garden with a small swimming pool and playground for children, a gymnasium, an open space for gymnastics, a 300-meter sprinters' track and a solarium with a snack bar. Also included were a number of service objects and equipment – "outdoor furniture" in the Le Corbusier sense of the word – such as concrete tables, an artificial miniature hill, flower boxes, ventilation chimneys, an outdoor staircase, and an open-air theater and cinema. All that, seen against the surrounding scenery, made a most absorbing landscape.

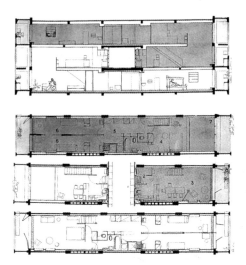

Unité d'Habitation: double-height living room (opposite page), photograph by Lucien Herve; section and plans through interlocking apartment units (left)

Unité d'Habitation: roof terrace paddling pool (above),
photograph by Lucien Herve;
sections (right)

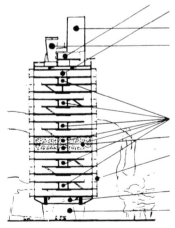

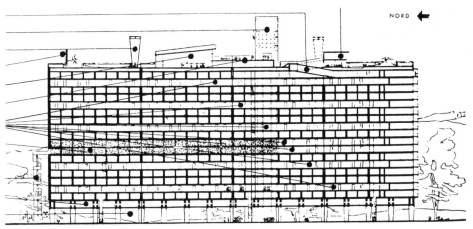

NORD ←

The building was constructed mainly out of reinforced concrete. To cast the concrete, Le Corbusier used rough timber formwork that left distinct traces on the surface of the structure – thus the name *béton brut* (rough concrete) to account for the ruggedness of its appearance. Given the impact of the Mediterranean sun, Le Corbusier employed for the building's facades the *brise-soleil*, which he had already developed for the Ministry of Education in Brazil and used also for the Algiers Marine skyscraper.

The Unité d'Habitation was Le Corbusier's most inventive and most influential project. As with most of his projects, the Unité was designed as a prototype and not just as a single case. Not only did it draw from his previous schemes, it was a condensation, a summa, and a culmination of research carried out over thirty years. The scheme evolved step by step and was worked out at different times and in different projects. It emerged like a new species out of a sea of evolutionary recruitment, recombinations, and mutations of L'Atelier de la Recerche Patiente ("the Atelier of Patient Research").

As with Le Corbusier's previous work, Unité d'Habitation demonstrates his elementarist, analytical approach. Compared to the traditional apartment buildings of the period, Le Corbusier's proposal appears unprecedented. However, as with most of his previous work, it emerged from recruiting, reframing, recombining, and redesigning precedents. Le Corbusier did not depart from the concepts of architecturally received routines. There was no entrance or lobby; there were no corridors, walls, windows, balconies, or roof. Everything was restated in terms of the most elementary functions the new product had to fulfill and the operations that could satisfy them. The project should not spoil the

Unité d'Habitation: *pilotis,* photograph by Lucien Herve

natural environment. The small living spaces had to be concentrated rather than letting them sprawl. In addition, this project had to touch the ground minimally. Unspoiled views of the unfolding grounds, light breezes blowing freely over the soil without being blocked, and sustained ecological conditions were also required. The project had to enhance the freedom of choice and lifestyles and had to offer a big variety of apartments of differing size and shape, unrestrained by the supporting structure. The inhabitants of the Unité had to help people enjoy the beauty of the striking "Homeric" landscape while engaging in open-air games and other cultural and leisure activities.

This is where Le Corbusier's analysis ended. The next step was to look into his thesaurus of precedents. He searched in his archive among the objects he had been collecting for years for those that appeared to have something in common with the object he hoped to conceive, which satisfied similar elementary requirements. He did not try to conceive a new kind of building ex nihilo.

Pondering how the new project was to relate to the ground without obstructing the soft Mediterranean winds and keeping the naturally unbroken surface of the earth, Le Corbusier's memory carried him to the ancient Swiss settlements, the huts built over the water on *pilotis*. Thus he developed the design of an immense slab building carried by thirty-six columns, which allowed the "ground to roll free" and "the gaze to pass" unobstructed under them. He was also reminded of the Roman aqueducts and their huge, concentrated linear mass extending in height and length over the countryside, touching the ground only at certain concentrated points, which "created" rather than "destroyed" the landscape.

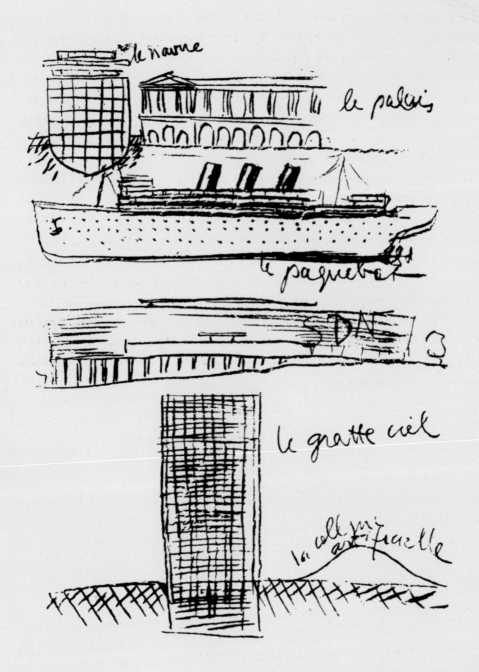

le navire

le palais

le paquebot

S D N

le gratte ciel

la ville artificielle

While wondering how the structure of the building would not confine the variety of apartments and choice of different lifestyles, Le Corbusier had the idea that this was like his bottle-rack, inside whose framework bottles of any kind, taste, origin, and age could be easily "shoved" in and stored.

While thinking how he could create a landing with panoramic views "opening onto a dream landscape," to make its "Homeric" beauty accessible for the inhabitants of the Unité engaged in "sunbathing," "tennis … games of all sorts," swimming, conversation and amusement, and "open-air hydrotherapy," Le Corbusier was reminded of ocean-liner decks, from which passengers can enjoy distant sights reaching as far as the horizon while taking pleasure from outdoor games and sports, while all the time "breathing magnificently pure air."

Once the specific precedents were identified in the aqueduct, the hut, the bottle-rack, and the deck, the next step was to extract them, to combine them, and recombine them into a new building with a known volume, *piloti*, structure, and roof. Certainly, this is a schematic diagram of how things might have happened. We have already described how Le Corbusier in his "patient research" not only collected precedents – he kept on producing solutions that he continued to recombine, refine, and redefine. In a phrase reminiscent of the great mathematician Henrí Poincaré's phrase to let problems be "hooked on the wall," Le Corbusier would let a problem "float," "marinate," "ferment." The Marseilles Block took almost three decades to be born.

Sketch comparing a palace, an ocean liner, the League of Nations, and a skyscraper

The Unité, however, is not just a new machine or a solution to a problem. If one accepts that, then its complexity, not to mention its dysfunctionality, remains unexplained, if not inexcusable. One cannot understand or justify why its appeal increases and becomes more universal as time goes by although it is just a crooked machine and a poor solution. Only one thing will account for this: that the building, as much as it operates as a "machine for living," works as a monument-metaphor for human life.

Conceiving of the Unité d'Habitation as a metaphor, Le Corbusier brought together parts from many unrelated objects, *objets à réaction poetic*, from sources that previously had been perceived as un-related, if not exclusive, into new ways of association and coexistence. Thus, the *pilotis* are not only to perform an ecological role. Neither is the giant concrete fire escape placed at the end of the block, with its obvious connotations of a boat's steering column, just to provide an emergency exit. Together, with the heteroclite objects – the bottles, the polychromatic cage-rack, the deck, the Acropolis top, (also viewed as an *objet à réaction poetic*) – they make new meta-objects that invite feeling and thinking.

"Life in a building is a journey on a liner" appears to be the metaphor implied by the scheme of the Unité d'Habitation. From the trivial analogy that life and journey have in common a beginning and an end, and building and liner are both containers of numerous entailments, judgments and inciters are generated. They do not tell any facts or utter instructions but rather, like a poem, a story, or a play, they frame settings and point to situations of human condition. Unité d'Habitation awakens to the predicament of postwar everyday life: the loss of quotidian joy, the dreariness of work, loneliness of leisure,

Plan and façade of Unité d'Habitation and ocean liner

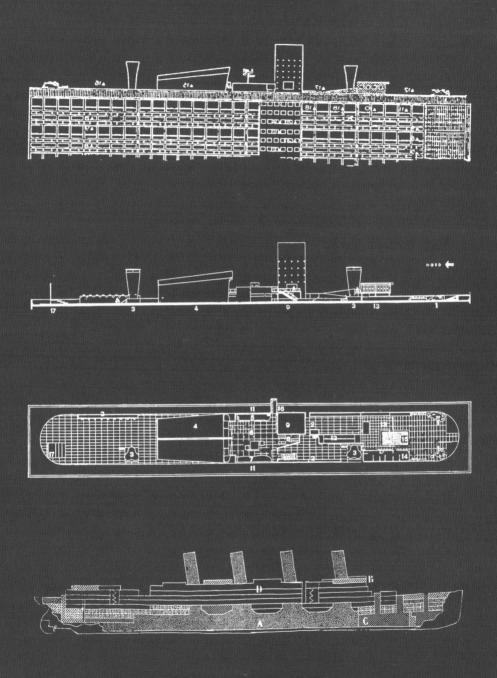

cheerlessness of learning, dissolution of community. Unité d'Habitation, in a very interesting way, was willingly self-contradicting. What it proposed and imposed as a machine for living, it dispossessed creatively to invite a new way of life. And that is exactly what makes the work such an enduring point of attraction and fascination.

Similarly, one can argue that the *béton brut* appearance of the Unité was a correction of the all-white appearance of prewar buildings. The white plaster used in the 1920s–1930s proved technically to be a failure. The facades stained and did not weather well. Thus, exposed concrete was chosen in the hope that it was going to behave better. The coarseness of the Unité, however, offended many critics at the time. Swiss, Dutch, and Swedish visitors to the building thought that the marks on its surface were defects of the material and a technical error. Thus, some of Le Corbusier's buildings, when executed without his supervision, were thought to need correcting of the defects resulting from constructing polished inferior buildings. Some visitors pitied Le Corbusier's failure to conceal the crudeness of the casting simply as a pragmatic submission of the architect to the constraints imposed by postwar austerity.

His aim, however, was quite different. The rough concrete of the structure was intentional. It was explicitly left bare in order to conserve the wavy grain patterns, the intricate arrangements of the fibers, the ribbons of tissue, and the cracks or fissures – the inside face of the wooden shuttering planks on

Unité d'Habitation: roof terrace

its exposed surface. Le Corbusier called these remnant wooden traces "wrinkles and birthmarks," and used them to create an aesthetic effect, or "contrast." With their "crudity," "intensity," and "spontaneity," they juxtaposed the extreme accuracy, detail, and perfection of modern construction technology. Beyond the experience of aesthetic contrast, the preservation of these defects – these "wrinkles and birthmarks" – appears to be a testimony of movement, recalling the liveliness of the hands and minds of those who creatively applied the technology of the times. In fact, the very terms Le Corbusier used, namely "wrinkles" and "birthmarks," are signs of the passage of time, the history of the human body. As with the ancones protruding from the masonry structure of Propylaea of the Acropolis of Athens, these traces were intended as witnesses of the structure's construction, the generative human performance and potential. Their "*non finito*" unfinished aesthetic quality implies the passing of time and the temporal existence of desires and aspirations of an epoch. They provide the means through which the Unité recorded its own history; together with the rest of its iconography it assumes what Ruskin called a "deep sense of voicefulness" and "mysterious sympathy" with the "passing waves of humanity."

Indeed, if Picasso's *Guernica* was in 1937 marking prophetically the coming of the war, the devastation, the slaughter of the innocents, the Holocaust, Le Corbusier's Unité d'Habitacion points to the ecological devastation, the destruction of the natural landscape and the decline of the sense of the joy of life. After the end of the war, Le Corbusier comes forth not only an engineer of machines for living but also as a maker of metaphors with which to think, an epistemologist, a moralist, and a dramatic poet.

Drawing from *Le Modulor*, Vol. I (1948)

"Landscape Acoustics" and "Light Canons"   **CHAPTER 06**

Le Corbusier was never faithful to a single project. As if having an architectural Don Juan temperament (compelled to carry on several affairs simultaneously), he pursued many projects at the same time, obsessed with each, but never dedicating himself to any one exclusively. There is no question that given the uncertain character of most of his commissions, that this was a necessary survival strategy. On the other hand, this behavior came out of a cognitive need for creative effectiveness: try several parallel paths in search of satisfactory solutions. Thus, none of his discoveries, whether they were materialized in buildings or not, were thrown away. Together with precedent solutions made by others, every new thought of his was carefully stored away to be reused if and when needed.

While Le Corbusier was working for the Unité d' Habitation in Marseilles he became involved with another Mediterranean project, **La Sainte-Baume**. "In about 1946, Édouard Trouin, a land owner from Marseilles, went up to Paris," Le Corbusier wrote in his *Œuvre Complète*. "There he visited everybody including the academicians," inviting them to propose an idea about "a project for the Val d'Aups at the foot of the Rocks." Trouin wanted to build in the midst of "this lordly landscape," as Le Corbusier called it, "a place of architecture, a place of meditation, a meeting place which would make possible the appreciation of the full value of the spirit which reigns here" and make "an architecture worthy of the countryside." No architect but Le Corbusier was responsive to Trouin.

Trouin came from a family of surveyors of Southern France that went back to the eighteenth century. By chance, or so Le Corbusier wrote, Trouin became the owner of a substantial piece of real estate, one million square meters of uncultivated land that, legend had it, was the divine cave associated with Mary Magdalene "guarded" in the 1940s by the Dominican brotherhood. As France emerged from the devastation of the war, new demands arose for leisure facilities. Those making such demands had very little to do with the elite high-class young generation for whom Le Corbusier had built villas and vacation houses during the 1920s and 1930s. These new clients represented a new phenomenon of mass, middle-class scale. People would come to the south, as close to the sea as they could afford, in search of a small lot to spend their vacations. A new set of opportunities arose, but also new needs arose. Shrewd entrepreneurs could see the possibilities of the tourist industry. Only a few sensitive people could see the hazards of destruction of the fragile Mediterranean landscape. Le Corbusier, as we have already seen, had made a statement about it while working in Algiers.

Trouin was also one of those few sensitive people. A self-made person, and an autodidact in many respects like Le Corbusier, he collected material on the history of art and religious legends about St. Magdalene and the history of the site and was fascinated with the visual arts. Instead of selling bits and pieces of his property, he saw himself becoming a developer, creating a megaproject that integrated with the landscape and combined the religious beliefs about it while enhancing its natural beauty. More concretely, he saw the possibility of a structure dedicated to ritual and contemplation, the **Basilique** in the rock. It would consist of a museum dedicated to St. Magdalene, two ring-shaped hotels, and the permanent city with related leisure facilities. More than a potential client, Le Corbusier had found a good companion with whom to dream.

The project was problematic in the context of the postwar situation in France. Unsurprisingly, it was received with tremendous opposition from all sides. Many felt it did not fit in during the time of austerity and reconstruction and that it impinged on the landscape. Trouin continued his efforts, modifying the program first with Le Corbusier and later alone, using Le Corbusier's name, which did not please Le Corbusier. Le Corbusier had to request for his name to be withdrawn. However, Le Corbusier referred to Trouin as his project collaborator, a title he would not easily bestow even to those who deserved it. Ragot and Dion remarked in their book about Le Corbusier that as years went by, the speculative character of the plan became increasingly evident. Le Corbusier, once more, was ahead of his times, in this case foreseeing the future of cultural tourism that would become a major business two decades later in Europe.

Trouin's unique property in La Sainte-Baume included a formidable wall of rocks on the edge of half a plate. The other half, slightly raised and looking to the north as far as the mountain Saint-Victoire, was known around the world from Cézanne's paintings. There is a series of fascinating drawings by Le Corbusier analyzing the morphology of the landscape. To preserve the profile of the skyline and exploit the dramatic impact of the panorama Le Corbusier conceived for the site, a Basilique as *chthonic* architecture. Le Corbusier's common strategy was to block a view initially, especially if the view was glamorous, to protect it from being devalued and habituated, leaving access to it only through a controlled opening. Here, hiding and revealing the view becomes a basic theme of the project implemented in a most dramatic manner. Shifting attention from the structure and the "skin" of the building to the interior, the Basilique was sculpted inside the rock rather than built on top of it.

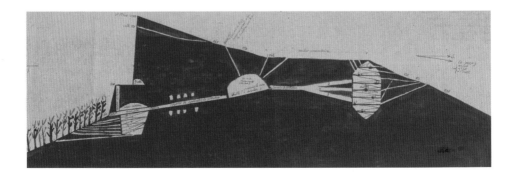

The scheme was worked out partially as pure interior, autonomous of the conditions of the outside and cut out of any view. The space was illuminated through specially shaped "canons" of light. In his *Œuvre Complète*, Le Corbusier refers to the precedent of the Villa Adriana, but the case of the light effects of St. Sofia was obvious. It is an *architectural promenade* run from one side of the rock at the entrance of the cave to the other, opening suddenly on the blinding light and the distant sea. The movement, however, offers not only a spatial experience. Emerging from the subterranean cathedral and the virtual space created by the Trouin displays and the control of light, one is exposed to the overwhelming reality of the blaring light, rediscovering the enormous sky and the distant sea. Le Corbusier recreated here an experience he wrote about in his *Voyage*, imagining the priest emerging from the dark adytum of the Parthenon on the top of the Acropolis, staring over the horizon of the mountains of Attica. "Inside mystery and twilight … and outside living people," he later remarked. Despite Le Corbusier's fascination with the idea of designing the Basilique, his project appeared to show no trace of religiosity or care for church symbolism. In Sainte-Baume, Le Corbusier tried to create conditions for contemplation, transcendence in an emotional and cognitive, rather than metaphysical, sense. Yet, the contemplation and transcendence he searched for here, in the cave of Mary Magdalene, does not seem to be very different from what he looked for in designing the wall with the small window within it for his mother's house on Lake Leman.

Accompanying the Basilique was a hotel facility, for which Le Corbusier and Trouin considered experimentally using aluminum, and the permanent "city," a small number of apartments arranged

Basilique, La Sainte-Baume, France, 1948

compactly in four rows. The plans drew from the 1920 Maison Citrohan and Maison Monol. For the apartments, Le Corbusier recruited the 1942 North African row housing of Cherchell where, in turn, he had reused regional Mediterranean spatial precedents adapted to fit contemporary operational needs and technological potentials. The Sainte-Baume scheme appeared as if the Unité d'Habitation "bottle-apartments" had been taken out of the rack and placed on the ground in order. This showed that Le Corbusier began to think about low-rise, high-density housing as an alternative to the high rise for reasons mainly of preserving the visual character of the landscape, saving at the same time the benefits of efficiency, ecological compactness, and social cohesion.

There was one more reason that Le Corbusier was so anxious to run after different projects, even proposing contradictory solutions as the Saint-Baume apartments appeared after his Unité d'Habitation. In contradicting himself, he manifested a systematic escape from any bounds that distance one from reality, even from his own beliefs. His stance against the mechanistic application of his own Modulor was well known, suggesting people to abandon it if it happened to contradict the facts at hand. The Saint-Baume scheme for the apartments therefore stands as a critical regionalist critique of the dogmatic application of the Unité of Marseilles and its mindless, technocratic, bureaucratic application. Unfortunately, not many architects paid much attention to this critique.

The experience of designing the apartments for Trouin fed the design of two other Mediterranean projects known as **Roq et Rob**, conceived and built between 1948–1950. The first project, Roq,

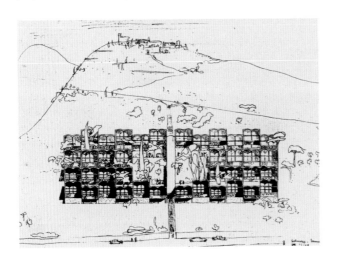

Roq, Vacation Houses, Cap-Martin, France, 1949

a sort of small country hotel consisting of separate pavilions, was situated at the flank of the steep hill at the little town on the Mediterranean Roquebrune, from which the name "Roq" was derived. The first sketches for the Roq were made by Le Corbusier on September 7, 1949, on the terrace of his favorite café, l'Étoile de Mer, while working with others on another project for Bogota. At that moment, Le Corbusier was staying nearby in the villa of his friends Eileen Gray and J. Badovici. As in the Trouin apartments, the scheme consisted of the repetition of parallel row units facing the Mediterranean. The notion of the street up in the air is reversed; here we have the high-density tower turned on its side with all units having physical contact with the ground. Each unit consisted of two stories covered by a vault, the dimensions controlled by the Modulor. The second study of Roq (1950) shows a "hotel in a crust," formed of minimal units serving all the needs of a hotel. A system of terraces replaced the corridors of the first version, each planted with citron trees. A system of stairs, underground passages, and an elevator made the units easily accessible.

Le Corbusier became enamored with the area and the café and felt very friendly with its owner, Roberto Rebutato. Two projects came out of this relation. One was a shed and the other, in 1957, was Rob, a very modest project on a very small terrain consisting of five minimal camping units on *pilotis* for his friend Roberto, after whom the work was named. Even in this very unpretentious commission, Le Corbusier wanted to make a general point. It showed that modern ideas about collective living, high density, industrialization, and standardization were not incompatible with living in contact with nature, the idea of the footpath, the "rustic," the shaded court, the character of the site, and the topography

Vacation Cabin, Cap-Martin,
France, 1950

of the region. And this, as we have pointed out above, while he was seriously involved with the conception, construction, and promotion of the radically opposed scheme for the Unité.

Le Corbusier has documented how he conceived his vacation shed, the "cabanon." Within three-quarters of an hour, he had sketched the plans on a table corner in l'Étoile de Mer, as a birthday present for his wife in December 1951. What was built differed very little from this first sketch. He started construction immediately the next year. Situated under the site of the Roq, the plan for the cabanon was a strict minimal cell for living, a house, a workplace, and a place for leisure all fused in one. It had a square plan with 3.66-meter-long sides and was 2.26 meters high. It took six months from its first inception to produce the construction drawings. Everything was designed to the smallest detail, including the furniture and the lighting fixtures. Contre-plaqué panels lined the interior walls. Le Corbusier tried other new ideas. One might expect that he would have designed by himself such an intimate project as the cabanon. Paradoxically, Le Corbusier decided to turn the production of its technical drawings into a collaborative process involving several specialists in his office. Once more, Le Corbusier was designing a new prototype, an experimental Unité des Vacances, a test he performed on himself and his wife very much like a doctor testing a new therapy first on himself.

Le Corbusier became the occupant of his cabin on August 5, 1952. In 1954, Le Corbusier finally ran out of space to live in. He had to add a workroom to the shelter a dozen meters away from it. Like a local Mediterranean, he built a studio without license, in the manner of a construction shed, and

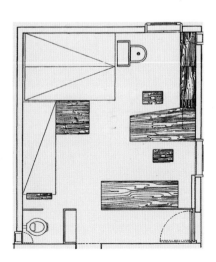

Vacation Cabin: floor plan (opposite page)
and Le Corbusier at work (above), photograph by Lucien Herve

Rebutato assembled it. Le Corbusier was so satisfied with the design and execution that in a 1952 interview with Brassaï, he said without a doubt he would end his life there – he did seven years later.

Many architects and artists of the 1930s saw in Le Corbusier, as they did in Einstein and Picasso, a model of the progressive man, a man of the modern, of the "New Times." For them, his involvement with the **Chapel of Notre-Dame-du-Haut, Ronchamp**, after accepting an offer in early 1950 by Canon Ledeur of Besançon on the recommendation of Father Alain Couturier of Lyons, came as a shock. Curiously, they were ready to dismiss Le Corbusier's ambiguous relations with the Vichy regime. They, like Charlotte Perriand, believed that "Le Corbusier was not a politician" but a visionary, a reformer, a technician who "was ready to make a pact with the devil to see his projects materialize." However, he was not doing so to satisfy any "personal interest" but to "transform life." Nor did they notice his collaboration with Trouin in La Sainte-Baume. Ronchamp was different. The combined effect of the program – purely religious, ritualistic, and devoid of any practical use – with the formlessness and inexplicability of the form – not only intractable to represent through basic geometry but also disguising construction – aroused negative reactions and, in some, even anger. The great twentieth-century historian of architecture, Nikolaus Pevsner, in his *Outline of European Architecture*, identified Ronchamp as the "the most discussed monument of a new irrationalism" that has a "movingly mysterious effect." And that was precisely why Ronchamp provoked such deep anxiety and extreme responses from all over the world.

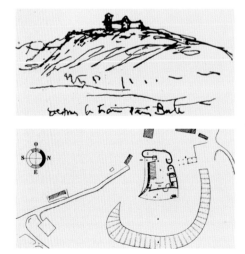

The ruins of the original Chapel at Ronchamp, Carnet Sketchbook 50 Paris-Marseille, 1950 (top); Procession to the Le Corbusier Chapel at Ronchamp, Carnet Sketchbook E18-Ronchamp, 1950 (bottom)

Chapel of Notre-Dame-du-Haut,
Ronchamp, France, 1950 (above),
photograph by Lucien Herve

Characteristic was the debate that opened in the pages of the January/February 1956 issue of the architectural review *Casabella*, between the art historian Giulio C. Argan and the architect (and director of the review) Ernesto Rogers. Rogers belonged to the 1940s–1950s generation and to those who reaffirmed humanistic values and individual expression, criticizing postwar reconstruction and radical attitudes that stressed materialistic comfort and centralized top-down planning in the name of rationality. He praised Le Corbusier's disruptive building as an effort to go "beyond the rational" – that is, beyond the standard, by then mainstream, approaches to reconstruction. And yet, in a complicated argument, he implied the building even went beyond the church's dogmatism.

Argan criticized Rogers for not realizing that by "going beyond," Le Corbusier had launched an attack against rationalism "defending the irrational." For Argan, "going beyond," or overturning a status quo, is the quintessence of rationality, and one achieves that through some new rationality and not through reverting to irrationality. Argan felt that Le Corbusier had undermined the "rationalistic European Utopia, the last act of an enlightened faith in the value of reason." What he found inexcusable was that Le Corbusier, the artist who was above religion, used capricious form, theatrical space, and hypnotic light and designed a "machine for praying" to "persuade poor plebeians to believe." Had the man who produced the "*machine à habiter*" begun to produce the "*machine à prier*?" Argan asked, worried that Le Corbusier was engaged by the Vatican. Today, such claims appear highly far-fetched. They are, however, indicative of the mood of the Cold War period and the struggles to construct ideological myths and appoint appropriate intellectuals.

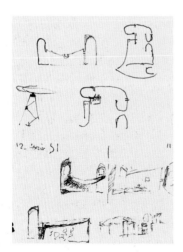

Carnet E18, numbers 319 and 320, 1951: conceptual sketches for the Chapel at Ronchamp (left); Chapel of Notre-Dame-du-Haut: east elevation (right), photograph by Michael Levin

In his publication, Le Corbusier celebrated the project: "1950–1955, Freedom: Ronchamp. Architecture totally free. No program other than the Mass services." The location has a very old history as a place of worship associated with a twice-yearly pilgrimage serving 12,000 pilgrims. For Le Corbusier, the requirements of religion had no major effect. The most significant constraint was the "landscape, the four horizons." As with Sainte-Baume, it became the driving force in the conception of the scheme that enforced the relation between new artifact and site. In the case of the Basilique, this relation led to a *chthonic*, carved-*in*-the-mountain "cave" architecture. In the case of Ronchamp, it led to a sculpted, grown-*on*-the-top, "summit" architecture environed by a landscape. As with the Unité of Marseilles, in the conception of Ronchamp, Le Corbusier recruited many precedents that were subsequently fused. The recruitment of the Aegean prophet Elias, churches were always placed on the top of a summit. Their plain, rectalinear, prismatic *megaron* form is translated into a boat, curved in ways to accommodate the visitors, protecting them from the wind and the sun. The resulting forms appear to echo the curvature of the land formations in the horizon.

Le Corbusier repeated several times the enigmatic statement that the configuration of the building was in "conformity with the horizons," "the acoustic response – acoustics in the realm of forms." The metaphor was the most obscure ever developed by Le Corbusier, yet at the same time perhaps his most perplexing and stimulating. It suggested that the building was conceived as a musical instrument, or that the building and its surrounding formations constituted a kind of huge concert hall. There are other precedents that also probably played a role in the configuration of the plan. As with Sainte-Baume,

Chapel of Notre-Dame-du-Haut: east
elevation (above), photograph by
Lucien Herve; view along south elevation (left), photograph by Michael Levin

Le Corbusier drew from his very early recollection of the relation between built volumes and the surrounding morphology of hills and mountains that he observed on the top of the Acropolis. The buildings might be rectangular, but the angles they define between each other, pointing inward or outward, acute or obtuse, are the equivalent of the convex, concave geometry of the walls of Ronchamp in dialogue with the folds and silhouettes of the surrounding ridges. Most certainly, the "spiral" approach to Ronchamp was also recruited from the precedent of the ritualistic helical procession to the Parthenon on the Acropolis.

North and west walls were concave and closed; south and east bent in. The three towers curved inside and out to form top-lit chapels or to offer niches into which sacristy and confessionals were set. An effigy of Our Lady was embedded in the east wall above the altar. The concave exterior of the east helps to project the priest's voice. More than any aspect of Ronchamp, the roof is a puzzle. Le Corbusier repeated several times that the idea came from a "crab shell" that he picked up in Long Island, New York, in 1947. The roof's structure and form, however, actually resemble a boat, and as the piers hold it up in the air, it looks like a group of men holding up a boat.

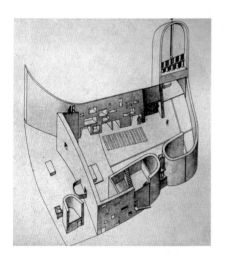 

Chapel of Notre-Dame-du-Haut: south wall window pattern (opposite page and above, right), axonometric from northeast (above and left), photographs by Lucien Herve

Maison Jaoul, Neuilly-sur-Seine:
France, 1952–1954 (above), photograph by Lucien Herve; plans
(opposite page) of ground floor (left),
first floor (center) and roof plans (right)

Not only the configuration of the building but also the surface appeared to be far removed from anything looking like a machine. But underlying the ruggedness and accidents of the skin was the finesse, precision, and numerical discipline of the Modulor. The same is true about the seemingly anti-mechanistic character of the **Maison Jaoul** in Neuilly-sur-Seine. This was a suburban residential project in a tight site surrounded by trees that Le Corbusier designed and built three years after the completion of Ronchamp, in 1956. A rather modest project, commissioned originally in 1951 by André Jaoul, an old friend of Le Corbusier, and his son Michel, it had an immense influence among young people around the world. Despite their numerous divergences of ideas, Le Corbusier's message was the same as Lewis Mumford's at that period. They both questioned what had happened to modern architecture, industrialization, and planning during the postwar reconstruction era.

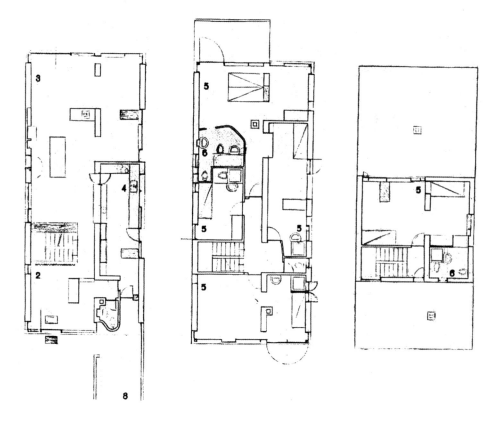

Dominican Monastery of Sainte-Marie
de La Tourette: Eveux-sur-Arbresle,
France, 1957–1959

In 1952, the provincial chapter of the Dominican brotherhood of Lyon commissioned Le Corbusier to design the **Dominican Monastery of Sainte-Marie-de-la-Tourette**. More than a church, a monastery expressed a commitment to a credo and a way of life, which both Le Corbusier and his colleague Iannis Xenakis felt was irrelevant to them, if not oppositional to their way of life. Le Corbusier was a descendent of the iconoclast *cathares*, who were defeated by Saint Dominique, the founder of the Dominican Order, which appeared to have found its reincarnation in the modern ideas of science and technocracy-based planning. In some parallel way, Xenakis appeared to belong to left-wing Greeks whose radical ideas had strong roots in the movement of the original Balkan iconoclasts. He was a political refugee in France, having escaped from Greece where he had been condemned to death for his political views. Like Le Corbusier, he was an atheist. He was educated as a civil engineer and was brought by George Candilis, another Greek political refugee rescued by Le Corbusier, to the office in 1947 to work as an engineer. Having done that successfully for some time, he asked Le Corbusier if he could work with him on a design project. Le Corbusier responded affirmatively, inviting him to work on a project of "pure geometry" – la Tourette. Later, issues of rhythm and light were also added to the problem. Both Le Corbusier and Xenakis took for granted the faith of the Dominicans and their style of life, which as professionals they decided to serve. Father Couturier, a person who played a very significant role in French culture after the end of the war, instigated the commission. His approach was part of a general effort of the Catholic Church in Italy, Germany, and France to revitalize religious art by introducing it to modern aesthetics. Irrespective of the particular faith of their creators, artists such as Henri Matisse and Marc Chagall carried out major works in this framework. Couturier, as well as Le

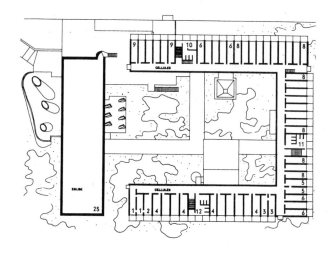

Dominican Monastery of Sainte-Marie de La Tourette: fifth floor plan

Corbusier, completely ignored that there could be a deep incompatibility between the presuppositions of modern art and those of the church. Religion was not discussed by either man, and neither did the monks touch upon the subject.

Interestingly, in the 1957–1965 volume of the *Œuvre*, the text accompanying the presentation of the project that contained references to the religiosity of the work was written by Jean Petit, a believer in God, and not by Le Corbusier. The symbolic elements that were entered into the scheme were not as an expression of belief but were elements inherited from precedents of religious architecture. In fact, the precedent of the "closed rectangle" atrium type was overtly "copied," as Xenakis wrote. It was not redesigned as Le Corbusier did with other precedents that he recruited from the past.

The building was designed to accommodate one hundred sleeping rooms for students and teachers, study halls, one hall for work and one for recreation, a refectory, a library, and a church. The complex sat on *pilotis*. The lower level was occupied by the refectory and the cloister in the form of a cross leading to the church. The study halls, work and recreation halls, and the library occupied the upper level. The loggias and the cells take the very top. The volumetric scheme resembled an inverted pyramid and drew from precedents of monastic architecture in the Balkans, especially Mt. Athos.

Le Corbusier faced two major problems in the design, both having to do with light. To control the light of the large communal spaces and the long passages, Le Corbusier arrived at the idea of

Dominican Monastery of Sainte-Marie de La Tourette: passage with modulor windows (left) and view over chapel light canons (opposite page)

"undulating" vertical glass panels. It was Xenakis who carried this rather simple idea into an architectural and formal innovation by developing a system of varying widths of the glass panels. Instead of any possible repetitive rhythmical motives, Xenakis applied the proportioning system of the modulor in periodic patterns of varying frequency or "densities" of points "on a straight line." His knowledge of systems of propulsion and modulation was the result of his knowledge of music as well as engineering and his contacts with the avant-garde music. The result of this fascinating interdisciplinary collaboration was not only a new spatial effect but also a new way of organizing rhythmically architectural elements in sequential order. Also with Xenakis, Le Corbusier developed the design of the light canons, which advanced the diffused lighting from above as was originated in Ronchamp. The collaboration between the two continued later with even more productive results. Xenakis's understanding of modern music and mathematics fascinated Le Corbusier, as those were two areas he always dreamt of mastering but never achieved. He was also intrigued by Xenakis's extreme moralism in politics, a kind of modern *cathare*, and, last but not least, by his lived experience with Greek traditional architecture.

Dominican Monastery of Sainte-Marie de La Tourette: view of chapel interior

"Drama out of stone"   CHAPTER 07

It was through an accident that Le Corbusier was offered the most prestigious commission of his life, **Chandigarh**, the plan for the new capital of the Indian State of Punjab and the architecture of its buildings. Plans for building the new city on the present site of a city began soon after the partition of India in 1947, when the old British province of Punjab was divided into two parts. India functionally needed a new administrative, commercial, and cultural capital for the inhabitants of what was left of the province after a large part of it became part of Muslim Pakistan and for the Hindu and Sikh refugees that moved in the area. It also needed a capital as a symbol of a new identity and a power that was taking over. Jawaharlal Nehru himself considered it a priority.

The precise location was selected by the end of March 1948. The new capital was to house 150,000 inhabitants and eventually would have 500,000 inhabitants. Political controversy followed the villagers of the immediate region who were in opposition to the government. However, P. N. Thapar, the chief engineer of Punjab, moved fast to appoint the New York civil engineer and planner Albert Mayer and his associates to develop a master plan by the end of 1949. Mayer was fit for the project. He had already considerable experience with India and the habitat problems of countries under development. Nehru knew him already from the time of the war. In addition, he was a close friend of Clarence Stein, the main creator of the housing experiments of the Sunnyside Gardens in Radburn and the Greenbelt towns in the United States before World War II. In his project, Stein developed an organization of settlements balancing nature and a modern built environment, pedestrian continuity and efficient motorized servicing, open plan and neighborhood structure. Mayer followed these principles in his

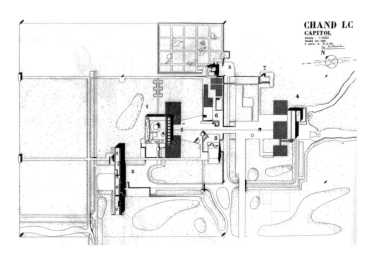

Plan for Chandigarh, India

Assembly and Secretariat,
Chandigarh, India, courtesy
Lucien Herve

Chandigarh plan, combing them with his local experience. He also introduced to the project Matthew Nowicki – recommended to him by Stein – the young architect who represented Poland in the discussions for the UN Headquarters in New York. Soon, Nowicki became involved, elaborating the neighborhood plans, with particular stress on leisure facilities, and designing building prototypes for housing as well as public buildings reflecting regional, climatic, and cultural context. By the middle of 1950, a schematic concept was completed and was ready for the approval by the Indian authorities. On August 31, however, Nowicki was killed in an airplane accident on his way from India to the United States.

P. N. Thapar and P.L. Varma, representing the Indian authorities, searched for an architect to replace Nowicki. In November 1950, Thapar and Varma came to the Atelier at 35 Rue de Sèvres. Le Corbusier, however, was not responsive. Their next step was to travel to London to meet with the British architects Jane Drew and Maxwell Fry who had worked already in developing countries and were involved in integrating issues of regional climate inside modern architectural thinking. Thapar and Varma asked them to implement architecturally the master plan across the lines already developed by Mayer. During the negotiations with Drew and Maxwell and following their hesitation to assume the responsibility of such an ambitious project, Thapar proposed Le Corbusier as an additional member of the team. To this, Maxwell responded, by "Honour and glory for you, and an unpredictable portion of misery for me." In December of that same year, Thapar and Varma were back in Rue de Sèvres. Le Corbusier accepted the offer, bringing in the project as an associate Pierre Jeanneret, who at that moment had broken from their partnership.

Chandigarh: conceptual sketch, 1952 (opposite page) and site plan (left)

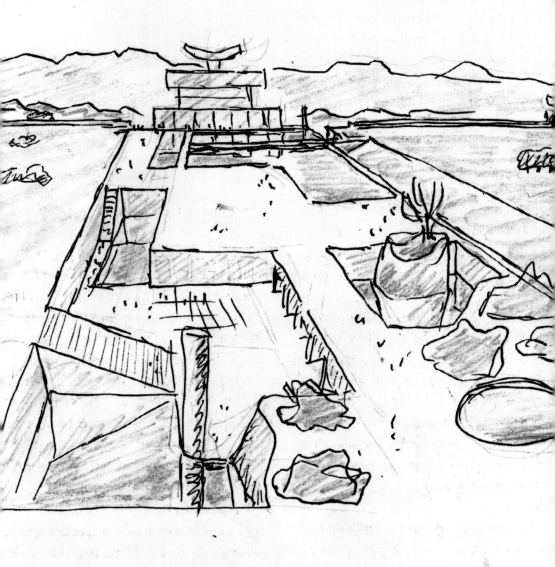

12 avril (2)
52

Predictably, Le Corbusier was not ready to follow the Mayer-Nowicki plan. His disagreement was not with the specifics of the Mayer proposal – most of his principles were actually later adopted in the end by Le Corbusier – as much as with the idea that he had to subjugate his design to another person's higher standing plan. Thus, in 1950, as soon as he was offered the design of the capitol building, he grabbed the opportunity and, in a typical move for him, settled to redesign the entire capitol before Mayer's arrival.

Le Corbusier was able to redo the whole plan in less than a month in March 1951. He could accomplish that in such a great speed because he was actually "correcting" Mayer's plan rather than thinking from scratch. In addition, his modifications were not new inventions but rather changes to make the plan adhere closer to the CIAM Charter of Athens with its elaborate over-analytical system of 7V's, the "seven routs," rather than to the more pragmatic Radburn Plan principles. Unfortunately, that had consequences that deprived the plan from the continuity of the green areas initially included in the Mayer proposal. Some changes, however, were highly personal. These introduced a monumental character to the plan stressing axial, compositional aspects as he had already done with his prewar proposals for Paris. They also involved the integration of the scheme in the landscape, the vast plateau between two great rivers, at the foot of the Himalayas.

Indeed the dialogue between natural formations and buildings is as dramatic as it was intended as Le Corbusier's drawings reveal and as Lucien Hervé's photographs manifest. The complex stands now as a giant work of art, a precursor of land art of the 1970s. Le Corbusier used the Modulor for the disposition of the buildings. From the social point of view, however, the plan is less acceptable. In dividing the plan into self-contained sectors, Le Corbusier reinforced the system of segregation of classes of the population as practiced in India, allocating to each sector a separate class.

Once the problem of the master plan was settled, Le Corbusier concentrated on the major public buildings while housing and the neighborhoods were designed by Fry, Drew, and Pierre Jeanneret along guidelines developed by Le Corbusier.

The **Palace of Justice** was the first building Le Corbusier designed for Chandigarh. Le Corbusier started working on it by 1951. It has been in use since March 1956. In no other built project by Le Corbusier does the viaduct precedent that fascinated him so much in his youth play such an important role. Within its colossal structure are inserted the various court and office functions. Le Corbusier tried to create a regional, "semi-tropical" envelope. The interior is protected on the two long sides by a 1.4-meters-deep *brise-soleil* wall, gently curving towards the outside as it goes up to provide shading as well as to protect it from the rain. The pattern is interrupted, leaving three pillows standing naked, forming a giant portico entrance. A huge roof, *parasol*-like, rests on the top of the structure shading its interior and protecting it from the rain. Maxwell Fry wrote that Le Corbusier developed the idea after Fry and Drew took him to see the Moghul ruins, pointing to him the microclimatic qualities of their design, "moving air under shaded conditions." Certainly, Le

Palace of Justice, Chandigarh
1951–1955, photograph by
Lucien Herve

Palace of Justice: elevation and ground floor plan, photograph by Lucien Herve

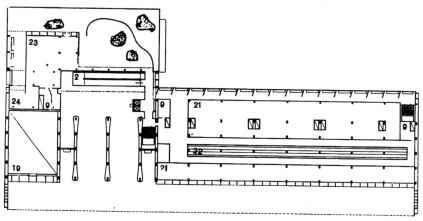

Corbusier had this idea much before he came to India and clearly tried it in 1928 for the Mediter-ranean Villa Carthage. On the other hand, the visit to the local architecture probably played a deci-sive role in congealing and adopting the parasol theme. Both parasol and *brise-soleil* are symbolic gestures acknowledging the spirit of the region, which was rather dysfunctional in their operation as climatic control devices.

To control the acoustics of the court rooms, Le Corbusier designed a total area of 650-square-meter tapestries. An enormous one for the "Great Hall" of the palace covering an area of 144 square meters (12 x 12 meters) and eight others for the smaller courts. Le Corbusier boasted that thanks to the Modulor it was possible to transmit the design in code by wireless from his Paris studio to India straight to the persons who were executing them, mostly prisoners and families of farmers.

Le Corbusier started working on the **Secretariat** in 1952. The building was finished by 1958. Its scheme – a 254-meters-long, 42-meters-high serial structure – drew from the precedent of the Unité d'Habitation. It contains ministerial chambers and all ministerial agencies. The sides are pro-tected from the sun by vertical *brise-soleil*, a system of "undulatories" made out of a total of 10,000 concrete mullions. Unlike the Unité, however, the units do not represent the outcome of any pro-found study of the workplace similar to the one Le Corbusier had carried out for the appartement. In addition to elevators and staircases, the circulation is accommodated by two large concrete ramps protruding in front and behind the building. The rooftop is used for receptions.

Secretariat, Chandigarh: entrance, 1951–1958, photograph by Michael Levin

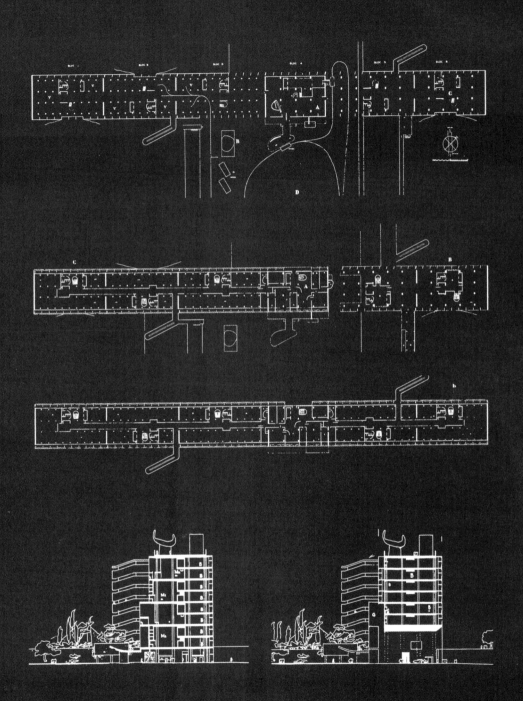

The **Palace of Assembly** took a longer time, from the day Le Corbusier started working on it in 1952 to the day of its completion in 1962. In comparison to the previously mentioned two buildings, it was the most complex. It included offices, rooms for committees and the press, a council chamber, and a main assembly hall. As opposed to the Palace of the Soviets, which had been designed by Le Corbusier at the dawn of his career and which followed the Villa La Roche prototype scheme (all functions independently expressed in an "ectoplasmic" manner), the Indian Assembly recruited the Villa Savoye closed, temple-like scheme. Yet, under closer inspection it appears to be a composite of four schemes, three Secretariats and one Palace of Justice all inscribed in a square plan leaving in the middle an atrium-like void to be occupied by the circular assembly hall, which was hyperboloid in volume. Inside the hall there is no speaker's platform. Each orator speaks from his seat and electronic devices were applied. The acoustic system was worked out in collaboration with Philips. The void left between the circle of the hall and the square was to be used as an informal lobby space dedicated to activities of informal social meetings and political "lobbying." The ceiling of the hall was designed to receive the winter sun, to reflect it in the summer sun, and to reflect the sun of the equinoxes onto the interior surfaces of the hyperboloid assembly offering to the politicians a feeling of cosmic participation.

Reusing the schemes of the Secretariat and the Palace of Justice was not the result of Le Corbusier's suddenly running out of ideas and repeating himself. It was clear that he was struggling to find a way of interrelating buildings in space to define a public setting, a sense of concordance and unity equally appropriate for the region, the cultural traditions of India, and the values of our time. As we have seen,

Secretariat (opposite page): entrance level plan (top), typical floor plans (middle) and sections (bottom), and sketch (right)

Assembly and Secretariat, Chandigarh
(above, photograph by Liane Lefaivre)
and Assembly (opposite page): elevation
(top), section (middle), ground and first
floor plans (bottom left and right)

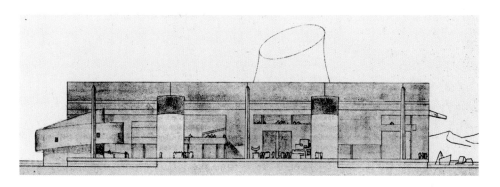

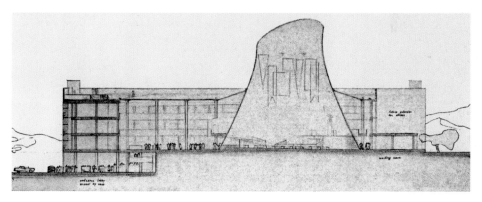

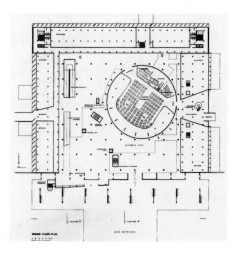

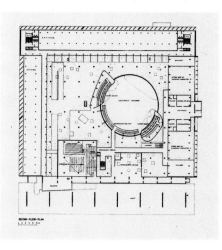

Shodan House, Ahmedabad, India,
1954–1957

Le Corbusier worked out theoretical urban schemes that included an area of public buildings since the 1920s. Chandigarh, however, was the first time that he was forced to take a stance, demonstrating in concrete terms how such a space was to be structured according to "modern architecture."

While Le Corbusier was involved with the Chandigarh monumental public buildings, he was commissioned a number of smaller, more intimate, private projects in Ahmedabad, the center of the cotton spinning industry. Despite their apparent novelty, most of the ideas involved a skillful, creative translation of earlier, prewar French schemes into a new regional, tropical context.

Thus, Surottam Hutheesing, secretary of the Millowners' Association, commissioned Le Corbusier to design his villa. When Le Corbusier finished with the drawings, Hutheesing sold them to a Mr. **Shodan**, the name under which the project is known. Shodan had another site for his villa, a fact that did not disturb Le Corbusier's plan. The villa was finished in 1957. The scheme, as Le Corbusier himself remarked, resulted by recruiting the precedent of the Villa Savoye of 1929–30. The square plan is encased in a sun-protecting, breeze-trapping cage of concrete walls. As in the Villa Savoye, an *architecturale promenade* is provided through a ramp that brings people up and down serving the various interpenetrating levels of the structure. Due to the climate the roof is not used.

During the same time Mrs. Manorama **Sarabhai** asked Le Corbusier to construct a villa for her and her two sons on her paternal estate, in Ahmedabad, Gujarat. The scheme is a kind of tropical version

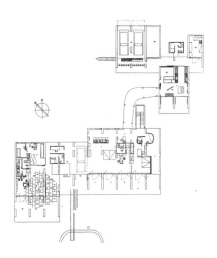

Villa Sarabhai: ground plan

of Madame Mandrot's villa. It was a deepened linear scheme made out of a series of bays to provide shaded gathering areas for living and entertainment in the midst of lavish growth. The bays are oriented to catch the prevailing breezes. The floor is of Madras stone paving, cut according to the Modulor proportions. Le Corbusier claimed that he saved material and applied it to most Indian buildings.

In turn, Surottam Hutheesing, who sold the plans of his Le Corbusier house, commissioned him to design the **Headquarters of the Millowners' Association**, one of the most prominent associations of Indian cotton mill owners that was on a piece of land on the banks of the Sabarmati River. Located in a garden, the building included central administration and the general assembly of the association.

The building includes offices and meeting rooms, an auditorium, a dining and lecture hall, and flexible places for unspecified cultural and social activities. Le Corbusier was given a flexible program for a business club rather than a formal institution. For him it was an ideal opportunity to develop one more prototype dealing with the problem that preoccupied him throughout his time in India, the application of principles of modern architecture to the regional, climatic, and socio-cultural constraints of a tropical location. As in the case of the Shodan House, the precedent of Villa Savoye gave the lead. The prismatic volume was pierced to allow ventilation while it was at the same time enveloped by multiple shading devices oriented according to the prevailing winds. The screen of diagonal fins of slender *brise-soleil* employed for the east and west facades, are parted to allow a ramp that started way outside the building and reached a vertical staircase that links the various levels of the structure. The effect

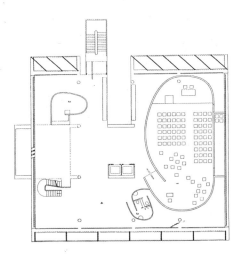

Headquarters of the Millowners' Association: plan level 4 (left) and photograph (opposite), photograph by Lucien Herve

of the *architecturale promenade* is dramatic, but its dynamism was achieved here, not without risks, as Le Corbusier provided stairs without a railing. In the sixth volume of his *Œuvre,* Le Corbusier stressed that opening the building at strategic places was intended not only for ventilation and shading. It was to take advantage of the situation of the building, offering a spectacle of the river and of cloth dyers washing and drying their cotton materials in the company of herons, cows, buffalo, and donkeys half immersed in the water to keep cool. The roof was used for evening entertainment.

If fate had not arranged for Le Corbusier to design and build Chandigarh, we would have had a different image of his work and accomplishments. It would have been one of an architect that, despite the immensity of his knowledge and capabilities, his contemporaries never trusted to offer him a proportionate opportunity to accomplish a real built project. Given Chandigarh, Le Corbusier was inscribed in history as a one of the very few architects who designed a capital and did so – to quote André Malraux's *Anti-memoirs* about his visit to the site under construction – designing it "down to the wallpaper."

On the other hand, ironically, if he had not built Chandigarh, in some respects our image of him would have been more related to exploration and innovation. Chandigarh, in many respects, looked backward. This is not referring to the efforts by Le Corbusier to reach back into Indian culture and history, noble efforts that were superficially carried out. It was more the general framework of architectural thinking that failed Le Corbusier to face the challenge of the situation. As mentioned already, apart from the investigations to provide a regional solution to the climatic constraints, the rest of the work did not add

Headquarters of the Millowners Association (left) and Secretariat (opposite page), both photographs by Lucien Hervé

to the thinking about public buildings and workplaces carried out during the 1920s. In addition, the treatment of the site as an urban problem remained imprisoned inside formulas of static composition without taking into consideration his own ideas about movement that became only an abstraction in a "plastic" composition. In India, Le Corbusier was lured by the call for a "new monumentality" of his own aging generation during the early 1950s. He blocked his own ambitions and those of the younger post-war generation for an architecture that provided a new way of life, a better human condition.

Functionally, neither the city nor the buildings were a success. The city failed in its provision of an adequate system of movement either for the pedestrians or for the vehicles. It also failed to sustain an adequate social life in its provision of services or facilities. It was neither generous nor controlling enough to accommodate persisting old uses or emerging new ones. The result became chaotic. Le Corbusier's climatic investigations about sun radiation, glare, air circulation, and humidity were based on illusory impressions and biases. The problems, of course, were immense. Without doubt, these were the most difficult problems Le Corbusier had ever faced. One could not expect one man or one workshop to have all the knowledge needed to resolve this. Many of these problems, however, could have been avoided if Le Corbusier was more open in observing the context within which he had to create as well as working out together with others the difficulties of the situation.

Le Corbusier was very eager to include in the center of Chandigarh a sculpture. It was a statement about India, the world, and his times. It was also a testament for the future. He chose the figure of the

Open Hand Monument, Chandigarh, India, 1969, photographed by Liane Lefaivre

open hand as the theme. The hand, as an abstract configuration and as a symbol, preoccupied Le Corbusier since his adolescent years. In his moving monument to Vaillant-Couturier in 1937, the monument had a prominent morphological and iconographic position in a complex of other elements. Independent of political beliefs that Le Corbusier did not share, Vaillant-Couturier fascinated him as a charismatic person involved in dialogue at the very moment the lights were going off in Europe. The hand for the Chandigarh monument was now the sole figure to dominate the landscape. It remains an inviting gesture rather than a declarative one, as in the Vaillant-Couturier monument.

In an interview before he died, Le Corbusier chose to comment on the Open Hand monument declaring it "not a political emblem," in the narrow sense of taking sides. It stands for the relation "of man to matter" and the realization that "everything is possible and that all conflicts can be diminished." Then he added "we must stop preparing for war … we must invent, enact works of peace … the Open Hand, open to receive … to distribute." Yet, it is ironic that in the very city he intended to erect this manifesto for dialogue, he carried out a solipsistic architecture.

Chandigarh suffered seriously from Le Corbusier's narcissistic tendencies of self-deception, his conviction that things were going to work out according to his intentions and that his buildings were to be understood without any questions as was intended by him who gave no explanations. As Doshi, the prominent Indian architect who worked for Le Corbusier during that time, said, "there was no dialogue" between Le Corbusier and the local people who in their admiration hesitated to challenge his proposals. "He did not ask; they did not question." Perhaps the process of designing these buildings would have been more cumbersome and longer if such a dialogue had taken place. But many of these mistakes could have been averted if more dialogue existed.

On the other hand, although Le Corbusier designed Chandigarh at a late stage of his life, in his sixties, this was not his last word on architecture. Very much aware of the views of a younger generation of architects unsympathetic with the search for a new monumentality, Le Corbusier was producing another architecture.

CHAPTER 08

By the end of the 1950s, a large number of important commissions arrived at 35 Rue de Sèvres from all over the world. Le Corbusier's "patient research" prepared him for this moment. He could comfortably recapitulate ideas and experiences, turning them into buildings, still claiming that his projects were original. Indeed, this is how he approached some of the projects of the later years of his life. However, this approach could not offer him the deep pleasure that only the cycle of exploration, struggle, and discovery and the bittersweet cycle of rejection and subsequent triumph could supply. Neither his collective *catharist* memory nor the memories of growing up with his family would allow that. In addition, Le Corbusier was also an author of his *Œuvre*, a historian of his own work but also of his times, and both roles demanded a different concluding chapter of his life project. The person who repeatedly declared that he was a revolutionary but whose form of revolution had to do with constructing new worlds by making people see the world in a new way could not rest on his laurels. Thus, while the two other figures with which we have compared him to before, Einstein and Picasso, appear to have slowed down searching for new prospects by the end of their lives, Le Corbusier seemed to be taking risks and experimenting with radically new ideas.

La Maison de l'Homme, Zurich, 1963–1967, photograph by Michael Levin

In the instance of the **National Museum for Western Arts** in Tokyo, Le Corbusier was finally offered the unique opportunity to implement an idea that went back to 1929. It was the spiral *architectural promenade* of "unlimited growth" proposed for an international center for science and education, the Mundaneum of Geneva. The spatial concept came back combined with the idea of a multidisciplinary cultural center during the period of the Popular Front in France, but it was never materialized. For the Tokyo project, Le Corbusier envisaged a building fit for manifesting a synthesis of the arts. With two Japanese architects who worked in his office as collaborators, Maekawa in 1928 and Sakakura in 1931, the Tokyo project was an enclosed volume sitting on *pilotis*, completely inward looking, with the contained space subdivisions forming a spiral pattern, accompanied by an experimental theater – the "box of miracles." It was a realistic implementation of an ideal schema. However, the excitement of an experimental, utopian character of the initial idea lost. And that was the danger of success faced by Le Corbusier at that face of his creative life that he did not escape in several of his late projects. Similarly, the **Le Corbusier Centre** in Zurich (1963–67), once more a building dedicated to the arts, was a materialization of an idea of an umbrella twin-roofed building that Le Corbusier had contemplated over the years.

Carpenter Center for the Visual Arts,
Harvard University, Cambridge,
Massachusetts, 1961–1964,
photographed by Eugene Lew

Also based on design elements, rules, and a scheme – as the Millowners' Building in Ahmedabad – was the **Carpenter Center for the Visual Arts**, which he had already developed for Harvard University, the only building by Le Corbusier in the United States. Joseph Lluis Sert, dean of the Graduate School of Design and one of the two architects of the Spanish Republic Pavilion for the 1937 International Exposition of Paris, where Picasso's *Guernica* was exhibited, approached Le Corbusier privately in a letter in October 1958. An official invitation followed. Initially, Le Corbusier resisted accepting the offer being busy with too many projects. Giedion, who was teaching at that time at Harvard, pressed him further by telephone to accept as an act of resistance to what Giedion called the superficial architecture that was produced at that time in America. To that, Le Corbusier responded sarcastically, asserting that he was not to assume the role of the "saviour redeemer" to what "Captain Giedion" wanted to assign to him. Sert finally won. He also became Le Corbusier's partner in the project.

Le Corbusier came to Harvard in November 1959 and stayed for three days at Sert's house studying the program, the site, and the way the collaboration with Sert was to be carried out. Le Corbusier received a very open program from Harvard, a basic reason being that the university expected him to provide creative suggestions not only for the building but indirectly for the educational program as well. The idea of opening the Visual Arts Center to the public of the university through the building was the university's. During Le Corbusier's visit, Jaqueline Tyrwhitt took him around Cambridge and pointed to him the flow of students, coming from their school located nearby, passing through the site on their way to the transportation center of Harvard Square. Thus, he decided to design an urban building

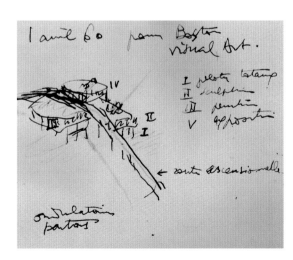

Carpenter Center for the Visual Art
conceptual drawing showing ramp

open to the public of the town rather than to the university only. As a result, instead of integrating his building to the collection of red-brick rectilinear volumes of landmark buildings of the campus by aligning it with them, he turned its predominant axis to meet the streets and the neighbouring building, the historicist Fogg Museum and Faculty Club, in an angle.

The Carpenter Center was conceived, more than any other project, as an *architectural promenade* open to the urban environment. An S-ramp links two parallel streets, starting from one street, climbing up, going through the building and ending lower on the other street. The five-stories-high volumes of workshops, exhibition spaces, and offices embrace this kernel ramp. They were made visually accessible from the ramp through the use of glass openings. As this ramp came to a peak, reaching the heart of the building, it was met by a second one linking it to the lower levels of the interior.

The overall idea of Le Corbusier was respected and executed impeccably. Perhaps too impeccably – Sert made certain that the building was executed according to the best American standards of finish. As in the case of the Tokyo museum, Le Corbusier's roughness of *beton brut* could not be tolerated. Dutifully, Le Corbusier characterised the resulted polished concrete surface as simply "too sterile." The most important change, however, was in the ramp system and the shape of the ramps. The idea of a second internal ramp proved to be too difficult to include. The ramps did not arrive to the ground as Le Corbusier wanted them, disrupting the connection with the street. On May 27, the building was inaugurated without Le Corbusier, who refused to attend for reasons of health and age, reasons,

Carpenter Center for the Visual Arts: site plan and floor plans
(opposite page), view of the ramp (left), photographed by Eugene Lew

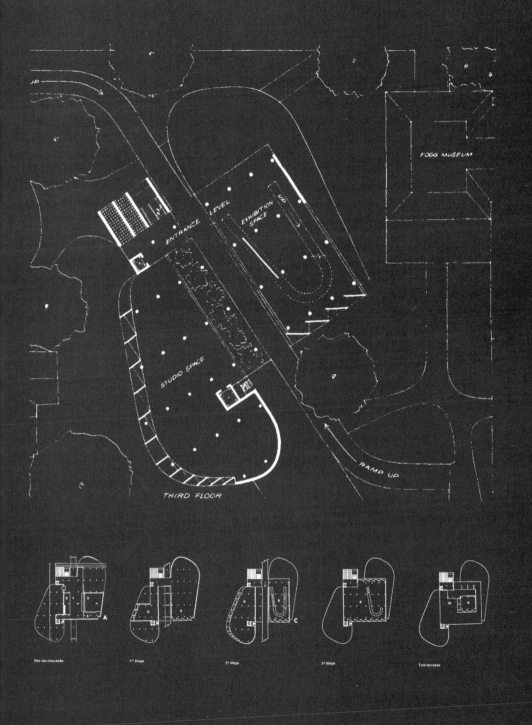

UP

FOGG MUSEUM

ENTRANCE LEVEL

EXHIBITION SPACE

UP

STUDIO SPACE

RAMP UP

THIRD FLOOR

Rez-de-chaussée   1ᵉʳ étage   2ᵉ étage   3ᵉ étage   Toit-terrasse

A   C

though, that did not prevent him from travelling to India. Again, more than a machine for carrying out a task – teaching in this case – the building became a metaphor for a place of learning, implying the dynamic dialogue between an internal and an external environment, an inside group and an outside onlooker.

In the beginning of 1956, the Philips corporation asked Le Corbusier to design a pavilion for the 1958 Brussels Expo. The **Philips Pavilion**, as it became known, was an unusual project. Philips was interested in a multimedia show, a work of art involving space, color, light, images, and music inside a structure. Its outside looks were not important. From the very beginning of the project, Le Corbusier thought of two people as collaborators, the composer Edgard Varèse for the music and Iannis Xenakis who worked in the firm, for the design and technical aspects. Xenakis composed also a seven-minute piece for the show *Metastasis*. Louis Kalff, a lighting specialist working for Philips and very much behind the whole idea, represented the client, coordinated the whole production, and made certain all tasks were accomplished on time. The contract was signed in October 1956. At a later stage, Phillipe Agostini was invited to be responsible for the montage of the images that were arranged by Jean Petit. The whole production was automated and remarkably no Philips products were displayed.

Le Corbusier developed very fast the first spatial concept by analogy to a biological organ, the stomach. People would enter, see, hear, digest, and move out. The architecture was to facilitate this movement and provide the environment for the acoustic and visual events to occur. Certainly, he had

Philips Pavilion, Brussels, Belgium, 1958: exterior views, left photograph courtesy Fondation Le Corbusier, right photograph by Lucien Herve

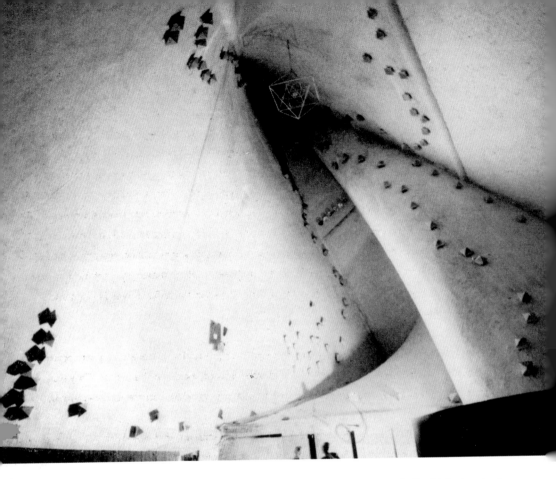

Philips Pavilion: interior view of roof
showing sound system (above), photograph by Lucien Herve; detail of suspended skin structure (opposite page)

already conceived shows involving media during his presentations of his ideas of the city in the 1930s. To some degree, the project resembled the *chthonic* architecture of the Basilique since it was a scheme without an exterior; only the going-through experience counted. To give it a tangible shape, he struggled with a bottle-like structure that was shaped like a stomach. It worked in plan, but it was difficult to envisage walls for projection and a roof over it. Iannis Xenakis proposed a tentstructure to be found in his structure of the 1937 Paris Fair pavilion where structure and surface were differentiated (as M. Treib remarked in his monograph on the project). For the Philips Pavilion, Xenakis proposed to develop an enveloping structural surface constructed geometrically out of shell segments in the shape of hyperbolic paraboloids. The solution was not only very efficient; from the point of view of structure, it was also conducive to simplifying the process of physical construction. Hyperbolic paraboloids were in the air at that moment. Felix Candella had been applying them with great success in Mexico. Matthew Nowicki had also applied them in Dorton Arena in North Carolina and in theoretical projects that were very popular.

Xenakis's use, however, was unique, applying with great sophistication to cover not a very simple ground plan. The walls were constructed of rough slabs in sand molds on the ground. They were mounted in place by means of movable scaffolding and were supported by a double network of cables.

There were many difficulties in resolving all structural problems, but they were finally overcome through the ingenuity and experience of a TUDelft professor of engineering, Vreedenburg and his

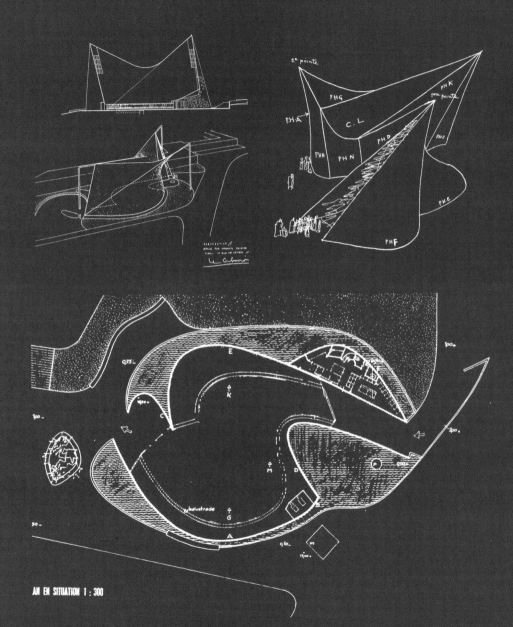

AM EN SITUATION 1 : 300

firm. What was not resolved, however, was the increasing tension between Le Corbusier and Xenakis. Xenakis demanded complete credit for his contribution as collaborator. Le Corbusier initially refused, but finally he accepted. However, in August 1959, he fired Xenakis by locking him out of the office without any advance notice. Xenakis stepped away from architecture to devote himself completely to music, and when Le Corbusier asked him to rejoin the firm a year later as an associate, Xenakis refused.

Whatever the contribution by Xenakis, Le Corbusier's achievement conceiving a "skin space" produced by a structure to contain a virtual reality environment was enormous. It was he who had the vision and took the risk at the end of a long creative life. To carry it out was a most innovative scheme, prophetic of an architecture to come, only at the threshold of the twenty-first century.

Philips Pavilion: conceptual drawings showing the plan and tent-like structure (opposite page) and interior projections (above), courtesy Fondation Le Corbusier

At the start of the 1960s, news appeared of a new project by Le Corbusier – the **Hospital of Venice**. It was meant for more than 1,200 patients and for more than 4,000 users. Moving away from the standard opinion at that time to design hospitals in vertical volume, Le Corbusier organized his project like the Frankfurt center, in three levels. The ground level was connected with the city and included general services and public entrances. The second level contained day-care services, special medical treatment, and the rehabilitation center. The third level was the main domain of hospitalization and included also a visitor's zone. In concordance with the average building height in the city, the total height of the hospital was around 13.66 meters; most rooms were 2.26 meters high. The facility was aimed for the seriously ill. The patients would stay for fifteen days there, out of which five were constantly in bed. Le Corbusier's plan provided for both phases, staying in bed and getting up and recovering. More than any building by Le Corbusier, the scheme was a diagram of an idea rather than a plan to be constructed. Many key aspects of the solution, such as the top-lit rooms without a view, the relationship between services and rooms, were questionable, if not unacceptable. Yet, as a diagram of an idea it was most significant.

In the beginning of the 1960s, this announcement of a new project by LeCorbusier was not earth-shattering news. This was not only because some of his latest projects did not seem to generate any new ideas but also because of a growing aversion for projects of plastic, formal, monumental character, qualities of many of the mainstream architects who imitated Le Corbusier, and there were many by then who appeared to be identifying with him. It was not fatigue but also the realization of the disruptive impact that postwar modern architecture had on human interaction, sense of identity, and

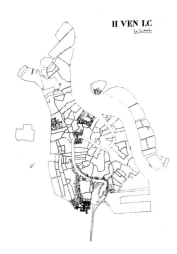

H VEN LC

Hospital, Venice, Italy 1964–1965: site plan
(opposite page) and plan (above)

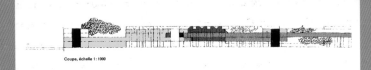

Coupe, échelle 1 : 1000

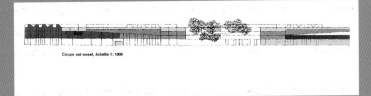

Coupe est-ouest, échelle 1 : 1000

Coupe, échelle 1 : 1000

Coupe est-ouest, échelle 1 : 1000

community. The young generation appeared to blame for that the high profile of sculptural, plastic architecture, the "universal space" interior, and the free-standing building. They asked instead for a return to the low-profile, "corridor" and "street"-based building that could sustain human interaction by enhancing physical contact. The most vocal group expressing these ideas was Team X. Interestingly, among the members of this group were three ex-employees of Le Corbusier – all three had been fired by him – Shadrach Woods, George Candilis, and Alexis Josic. Their ideas were expressed in writings and lectures, but most importantly in competition projects. One of them was the submission for the re-construction of the Centre of Frankfurt. Woods, who like the others, continued to be friendly with Le Corbusier, decided to show to Le Corbusier the plans for this project. Le Corbusier was struggling at that moment with the Venice Hospital. Placed off the center, on the northwest edge of the narrow island of the historic town, the site was still very sensitive for any free-standing, sculptural building. Le Corbu-sier accepted to have a look at the plans and asked Woods to come by the next day. That day Le Corbu-sier gave the Woods plans to his assistants almost telling them that *they* were his plans of the hospital.

Woods told me this story personally, which was subsequently confirmed to me by Julian his chief assis-tant, when I exhibited the project at Harvard after Le Corbusier's death. Did Le Corbusier steal the idea? Neither Woods nor Julian believed so. It was his clumsy, tortured, and never learned way of doing work in dialogue, a basic condition at that moment for accomplishing a creative leap. Thus, although Le Corbu-sier claimed that he conceived his hospital by respecting the Venice project, it was more the result of his reaction to the new situation in architecture, to the new challenges of the times, the new "New Times."

Hospital, Venice: sections

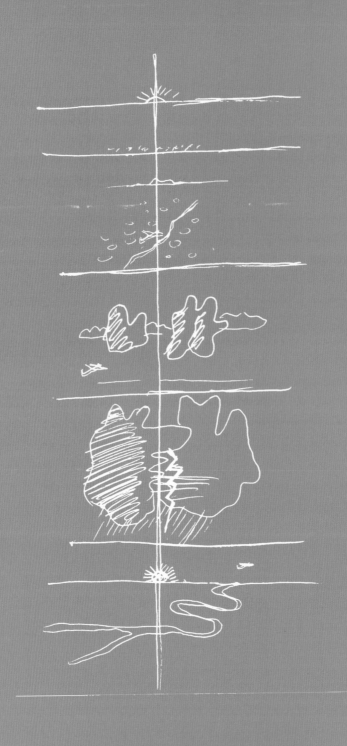

"Everything Returns to the Sea"

When Le Corbusier declared that *"everything is architecture,"* his intention was to redesign architectural beliefs and desires that dominated professional thinking of designers and users of buildings and cities at the beginning of the twentieth century. It was a very ambitious global program that involved making artifacts and environments with the aim to enable activities; embody meanings; and imply actions, that is encompassing physical as well as symbolic functions in the broadest sense. None of the architects of his generation were able to conceive and fulfill such a program as Le Corbusier did leading to a unique, new poetics of *machine* and *metaphor*. It is justifiable therefore to claim that only Le Corbusier merits the designation of the *architect* of *modern life*. Following that, one is tempted to ascertain further that Le Corbusier was a miraculous, charismatic person who forced upon his contemporaries some personal vision of the world and, paraphrasing a saying about Plato and philosophy, to pronounce that after him the achievements of other architects are only a footnote.

A historian's study of Le Corbusier shows something different. His achievements were a product of a long – one might use here an architectural metaphor – design and construction process. During this process, very special gifts of *spatial intelligence*, personal drives emergent out of family conflicts and bonds, perceived needs and aspirations built within the collective memory of his hometown, as well as historical circumstances, necessities, and possibilities of his time, were combined within a long process of cognitive development. Reflecting on this process, Le Corbusier called it "patient research." The "research" started as we have seen, by putting into action his postulate that "to see is to discover, to invent." That involved an intensive collection of precedents, "*objets trouvés*," which he called objects "*à réaction poétique*." One can paraphrase that by saying that those were objects pregnant with potential new meanings that could be re-categorized and recruited in creative making to "forge the tools of an epoch." Within a short period of a decade and a half he tried these new design tools – actually a collection of elements, rules, and types such as the *pilotis*, the "dom-ino" frame, the "free plan," the roof garden – to different kinds of buildings – "palaces, sea-scrapers, and Virgilian dreams." He kept on constructing these tools, recombining, changing, and modifying them to fit better to emerging technological, social, and cultural conditions by adaptation and selection in a manner resembling natural evolution. His efforts to try them on the scale of the city were met by the arrival of World War II and the crisis that preceded it. Le Corbusier called the war years a period "between the sum of errors and the dawn of renewal." It was during this period that what characterized his singular intelligence, both inherent and acquired through his "research," also showed its flaws. Le Corbusier's ability to perform by analysis and analogy major leaps of innovation blinded him to the moral problems posed by the advancement of totalitarian regimes and the war. He looked at the task of the construction of a better life within a better habitat as a long-term project that went beyond the war that he thought was only a temporary crisis. After the war, in the period of reconstruction he recruited once more his objects "*à réaction poétique*," "huts, bottle-racks, liners," to create the new "*unité*." The project of constructing a new way of making architecture was continued exploration of new environmental tools, such as "landscape acoustics" or the "light canons," and trying them in institutional buildings or in larger settings as in the "geometric event of on the plain"

Unité d'Habitation, Nantes, France, photographed by Lucien Hervé

of Chandigarh. However, his compartmentalization of thinking resulted several times in moral indifference. This subsequently blocked the new; bred illusions and biases; and caused unanticipated, unintended, and unwanted failures. Thus, Le Corbusier as the *architect* of *modern life* tells us much about the power and constraints of creativity as well as the fiascos and achievements of the twentieth century.

Then, as his biological powers were in decline, Le Corbusier's habit of the mind to seek survival through innovation led him to a new creative phase constructing once more new design tools. His architecture of "Cartesian Spirit," much closer to the original spirit of Descartes than his earlier experiments with high-rise buildings he called Cartesian. It resembles the Descartes Method in that it was developed in a period of great upheavals, confrontations with alien cultures, inventions of new instruments, and collisions with strange data. Opting for the certain, the graspable, and the simple, it proposed a minimal structure of thinking and guaranteeing the gradual but steady replacement of old ideas by new ones. During the end of his life, Le Corbusier appears to react to the disruptive impact of postwar modern architecture on community and to its inability to cope with increasing demands for change and choice. In key projects of the last decade of his life, such as the Philips Pavilion and the Venice Hospital, he developed design tools to expand human communication, introducing new multimedia virtual environments within the old confines of the building and a movement of organization to sustain human interaction. The building is not a finite composition. It is an open minimal structure, an epigenetic landscape where "everything returns to the sea," taking its natural path. Environmental choices are left free to emerge and develop open to the future and to the people who will live within it and with it.

BIBLIOGRAPHY

Benton, T., (1987) *The Villas of Le Corbusier 1920–1930*, Yale University Press, New Haven, Ct.

Besset, M., (1968) *Qui était Le Corbusier?*, Skira, Genève.

———, (1976) *Le Corbusier*, Rizzoli, New York.

Brady, D., (1985) *Le Corbusier, an Annotated Bibliography*, Garland, New York, London.

Brooks, H. Allen, (1997) *Le Corbusier's Formative Years*, University of Chicago Press, Chicago, Ill.

Chiambretto, B., (1987) *Le Corbusier à Cap-Martin*, series Monographies d'architecture, Éditions Paranthèses, Marseille.

Cohen, Jean-Louis, (1987) *Le Corbusier et la mystique de l'URSS; theories et projets pour Moscou, 1928–1936*, Mardaga, Bruxelles.

Curtis, W. J. R., (1986) *Le Corbusier, Ideas and Forms*, Phaidon Press Ltd., London.

Dudley, G. A., (1994) *A Workshop of Peace; Designing the United Nations Headquarters*, MIT Press, Cambridge, Mass.

Evenson, Norma, (1966) *Chandigarh*, University of California Press, Berkeley, Calif.

Fishman, Robert, (1977) *Urban Utopias in the Twentieth Century*, Basic Books, New York.

Frampton, Kenneth, (2001) *Le Corbusier*, Thames & Hudson, London.

Fuchs, W. and Wischer, R., (1985) *H VEN LC; Le Corbusiers Krankenhausprojekt für Venedig*, Dietrich Reimer Verlag, Berlin.

Gans, Deborah, (1987) *The Le Corbusier Guide*, Princeton Architectural Press, Princeton, N.J.

Gauthier, Maximilien, (1944) *Le Corbusier ou l'architecture au service de l'homme*, Denoël, Paris.

Gresleri, Giuliano, (1979) *L'esprit nouveau: Parigi–Bologna costruzione e ricostruzione di un prototipo dell' architettura moderna*, Electa Editrice, Milan.

Gubler, Jacques, (1987) *Le Corbusier; Early Works by Charles-Edouard Jeanneret-Gris*, St. Martin's Press, New York.

Henze, Anton, (1963) *Le Corbusier, La Tourette; Le Corbusier's erster Klosterbau*, Keller, Starnberg.

Hervé, Lucien, (1970) *Le Corbusier: As Artist, As Writer*, Éditions du Griffon, Neuchatel.

Jencks, Charles, (1973) *Le Corbusier and the Tragic View of Architecture*, Harvard University Press, Cambridge, Mass.

———, (2000) *Le Corbusier and the Continual Revolution in Architecture*, Monacelli Press, N.Y.

Jenger, Jean, (1993) *Le Corbusier; l'architecture pour émouvoir*, Découvertes Gallimard, Paris.

Jullian de la Fuente, Guillermo, (1968) *The Venice Hospital Project of Le Corbusier*, Wittenborn, New York.

Kaufman, Emil (1933) *Von Ledoux bis Le Corbusier; Ursprung und Entwicklung der Autonomen Architektur*, Verlag Dr. Rolf Passer, Vienna.

Le Corbusier (1950) *L'Unité d'Habitation de Marseille*, Le Point, Souillac.

———, (1997) *The Final Testament of Père Corbu*, a translation and interpretation of *Mise au Point* by Ivan Zaknic, Yale University Press, New Haven, Ct.

Lucan, J., (1987) *Le Corbusier, une encyclopédie*, Editions du Centre Pompidou, (collections Monographie), Paris.

Moos, Stanislaus von, (1979) *Le Corbusier: Elements of a Synthesis*, translated by Beatrice Mock, Joseph Stein, and Maureen Oberil, MIT Press, Cambridge, Mass.

Papadaki, S., editor, (1948) *Le Corbusier: Architect, Painter, Writer*, Macmillan, New York.

Pauly, Danièle, (1997) *Le Corbusier: La chapelle de Ronchamp*, Fondation Le Corbusier, Paris & Birkhäuser Publishers, Basel.

Petit, Jean, (1970) *Le Corbusier, lui-même*, Forces-Vives, Editions Rousseau, Genève.

Ragot, G. & Dion, M., (1987) *Le Corbusier en France; projets et réalisations*, Electa, Milan, Paris.

Sbriglio, Jaques (1992) *Le Corbusier: L'Unité d'habitation de Marseille*, Éditions Parenthèses, Marseille.

Sekler, E. F. & Curtis, W., (1978) *Le Corbusier at Work, The Genesis of the Carpenter Center for the Visual Arts*, Harvard University Press, Cambridge, Mass.

Serenyi, P., (1975) *Le Corbusier in Perspective*, Artists in Perspective series, Prentice-Hall, Englewood Cliffs, N.J.

Taylor, Brian Brace, (1980) *Le Corbusier; la Cité de refuge, Paris 1929–1933*, Équerre, Paris.

Treib, M., (1996) *Space Calculated in Seconds: The Philips Pavillion, Le Corbusier, Edgard Varèse*, Princeton University Press, Princeton, N.J.

Turner, Paul V., (1977) *The Education of Le Corbusier*, Garland, N.Y.

Viatte, G., (1987), *Le Corbusier et la mediterranee*, Éditions Paranthèses, Marseille.

Vogt, A. M., (1998) *The Noble Savage, Toward an Archaeology of Modernism*, MIT Press, Cambridge, Mass.

Walden, Russell, (1977) *The Open Hand: Essays on Le Corbusier*, MIT Press, Cambridge, Mass.

BOOKS BY LE CORBUSIER

Jeanneret-Gris, Charles-Edouard (Le Corbusier), (1912) *Étude sur le mouvement d'art décoratif en Allemagne*, Haefeli & Cie, La Chaux-de-Fonds.

_____, (1918) *Aprés le cubism*, Paris.

_____, (1923) *Une petite maison, 1923*, Le Carnet de la recherche patient, n. 1, Girsberger, Zürich.

_____, (1924) *Vers une architecture*, G. Crès et Cie, Paris.

_____, (1925) *L'art décorative d'aujourd'hui*, G. Crès et Cie, Paris.

_____, (1928) *Une maison – un palais*; "À la recherche d'une unité architecturale," G. Crès et Cie, Paris.

_____, (1929) *The City of Tomorrow and Its Planning*, Payson & Clarke, New York.

_____, (1930) *Précisions sur un état présent de l'architecture et de l'urbanisme*, G. Crès et Cie, Paris.

_____, (1933) *Croisade, ou, le crépescule des académies*, G. Crès et Cie, Paris.

_____, (1935) *Aircraft*, The Studio, Ltd., London.

_____, (1935) *La ville radieuse, éléments d'une doctrine d'urbanisme pour l'équipment de la civilisation machiniste*, Éditions de l'Architecture d'Aujourd'hui, Boulogne.

_____, (1938) *Des Canons, des Munitions? Merci! Des logis ... S.V.P. ... Pavillon des Temps Nouveaux*, Éditions de l'Architecture d'Aujourd'hui, Boulogne (Seine).

_____, (1942) *Le modulor, essai sur une mesure harmonique à l'echelle humaine applicable universellement à l'architecture et à la mécanique*, Éditions de l'Architecture, Paris.

_____, (1942) *Les maisons "murondins,"* E. Chiron, Paris.

_____, (1943) *La charte d'Athènes*, Plon, Paris.

_____, (1945) *Les trois établissements humains*, Collection ASCORAL sections 5a and 5b: Une civilisation du travail, 7, Denoël, Paris.

_____, (1947) *The Four Routes*, Dennis Dobson, London.

_____, (1948) *Le Modulor*, Paris.

_____, (1948) *New World of Space*, Reynal and Hitchcock, New York.

_____, (1950) *Le Modulor 2*, Paris.

_____, (1950) *Poésie sur Alger*, Falaize, Paris.

_____, (1950) *Unité d'habitation à Marseille de Le Corbusier*, Le Point, Mulhouse.

_____, (1953) *The Marseilles Block*, Harvill Press, London.

_____, (1955) *Poème de l'angle droit*, Tériade, Paris.

_____, (1957) *The Chapel at Ronchamp*, Praeger, New York; Architectural Press, London.

_____, (1958) *Le poème électronique, Le Corbusier*, Éditions de Minuit.

_____, (1960) *Creation is a Patient Search*, Praeger, New York.

_____, (1960) *L'atelier de la recherche patiente*, Vincent, Fréal et Cie, Paris.

_____, (1966) *Le voyage d'Orient*, Éditions Forces-Vives, Paris.

_____, (1966) *Mise au point*, Éditions Forces-Vives, Paris.

_____, (1968) *Dessins*, Éditions Forces Vives, Paris, Geneva.

_____, (1973) *The Athens Charter*, Grossman, New York.

Le Corbusier Sketchbooks, in 4 volumes, edited by A. Wogensky and F. de Franclieu, MIT Press, Cambridge, Mass.

Œuvre Complètes, 1910–1965, published in 8 volumes, edited by Willy Boesiger, 1st volume co-edited with O. Stonorov, 3rd volume edited by Max Bill, Girsberger, Zürich, 1930–1971.

The Le Corbusier Archive, in 32 volumes, edited by Allen H. Brooks, The Garland Architectural Archives, General Editor Alexander Tzonis, Garland, New York, 1982–1984.